SUICIDE
FROM A PSYCHOLOGICAL
PERSPECTIVE

SUICIDE
FROM A PSYCHOLOGICAL
PERSPECTIVE

By

DAVID LESTER

Professor of Psychology
Richard Stockton State College
Pomona, New Jersey

CHARLES C THOMAS • PUBLISHER
Springfield • Illinois • U.S.A.

Published and Distributed. Throughout the World by
CHARLES C THOMAS • PUBLISHER
2600 South First Street
Springfield, Illinois 62794-9265

© *1988 by* CHARLES C THOMAS • PUBLISHER
ISBN 0-398-05489-4
Library of Congress Catalog Card Number: 88-4941

With THOMAS BOOKS *careful attention is given to all details of manufacturing
and design. It is the Publisher's desire to present books that are satisfactory as to their
physical qualities and artistic possibilities and appropriate for their particular use.*
THOMAS BOOKS *will be true to those laws of quality that assure a good name
and good will.*

Printed in the United States of America
Q-R-3

Library of Congress Cataloging in Publication Data
Lester, David, 1942-
    Suicide from a psychological perspective/by
David Lester.
        p. cm.
    Includes bibliographies and index.
    ISBN 0-398-05489-4
    1. Suicide—Study and teaching. 2. Suicide—
Psychological aspects. I. Title.
        [DNLM: 1. Suicide—psychology. HV 6545 L641s]
HV6545.L425 1988
616.85'8445—dc19
DNLM/DLC
for Library of Congress   88-4941
                                                                        CIP

For Abraham Maslow...
who encouraged me and allowed me to grow

CONTENTS

SUICIDE
FROM A PSYCHOLOGICAL
PERSPECTIVE

Chapter 1

INTRODUCTION

IT IS interesting to compare the position of suicide as a topic for study in the disciplines of psychology and sociology. Broadly speaking, suicide has the status of an important topic and is considered relevant to basic theories of sociology. In contrast, suicide is not considered an acceptable topic for study in psychology and is ignored by psychological theories.

Such a statement needs some documentation. In sociology, one of the important theorists in the development of the discipline was Durkheim (Turner and Beeghley, 1981). As part of his heritage, Durkheim (1951) devoted one of his books to the topic of suicide. The concepts that he employed in providing an explanation for suicide, anomie and egoism, have become central concepts in sociological theory, especially anomie.

Deviant behavior is a standard course in sociology departments, and suicide is properly included in the range of the course. The leading sociology journals (the *American Journal of Sociology* and *American Sociological Review*) publish articles on suicide that are important for a theoretical understanding of suicide and which make important empirical contributions to our understanding of suicide. For example, mention might be made of Phillips's (1982) important work on imitation in suicide, Gibbs's (1982) research on his status integration theory and the recent article by Pescosolido and Mendelsohn (1985) on the effect of medical examiner office characteristics on the societal correlates of suicidal behavior.

It is also true that sociologists have proposed the most comprehensive theories of suicide, beginning with Durkheim, and proceeding with Henry and Short (1954) and Gibbs and Martin (1964).

When we turn to psychology, we see a very different picture. First, none of the major theorists who have contributed to the discipline ever focussed on suicide. Freud, whose work was most seminal to the discipline, did of course mention suicide, but his ideas on the topic were not collected together systematically until Litman (1967) undertook the task. After Freud, few theorists have mentioned suicide, even in passing. Why?

Psychology in the USA quickly became empirical, demanding individual studies of subjects. In addition, preference was given to the study of phenomena which could be artificially simulated in the laboratory. To be sure, some psychologists studied memory, for example, in the way that it occurs in people living normal lives (for example, Bartlett, 1932). But preference has always been given to studying memory of artificial material presented in the laboratory. Furthermore, the preferred technique for psychological research is the experiment, in which the experimenter manipulates independent variables to explore their effect on some dependent variable.

Suicide is not amenable to these preferred techniques of study. The suicide is dead and so no longer available for study. It is hard to conceive of a laboratory analog of suicidal behavior, and it would most certainly be seen as unethical to manipulate stimulus conditions so as to produce self-destructive behavior in people.

In course content, the course most clearly pertinent to suicide is Abnormal Psychology, the study of psychological disturbance. In this, the orientation has always been tied to diagnoses, closely following decisions made by the American Psychiatric Association. Abnormal Psychology textbooks are almost always oriented around the Diagnostic Manual of the American Psychiatric Association. In the 1970s, there would be chapters on neuroses, psychoses, psychosomatic illnesses, organic mental disorders, etc. Now, the chapters follow the new diagnostic categories, such as anxiety disorders, affective disorders, etc.

Lone voices occasionally argue for the study of meaningful behaviors (such as hallucinations or suicide) rather than diagnostic labels (Persons, 1986), arguing that we might learn much more about human behavior in this way (rather than learning about a diagnostic system that may be abandoned in a few years). These voices are ignored.

In Abnormal Psychology textbooks, suicide is typically placed in the chapter on affective disorders, where one can read an article that might be suitable for a Sunday newspaper magazine section.

What about the journals? The leading journal relevant to suicide published by the American Psychological Association is the *Journal of Abnormal Psychology*. Only rare articles appear on suicide there, and usually they are of poor quality, probably owing the lack of experience of psychologists in reviewing research on the topic. For example, one of the few articles published in the 1980s in the journal on suicide reported a follow-up of gifted individuals in the Terman cohort who had killed themselves (Tomlinson-Keasey, et al., 1985). However, the authors omitted to include a cohort matched for the degree of psychological disturbance, and so their results may be summed up as "those who kill themselves are more psychiatrically disturbed than those who do not," a conclusion that we could have drawn at least fifty years ago. A recent study in the other journal that publishes research on suicide, the *Journal of Consulting and Clinical Psychology*, compared the scores of a group of attempted suicides on an obscure psychological test to norms for the test (Mehrabian and Weinstein, 1985), again the omission of a simple control group.

It might be that psychiatrists could come to the aid of psychologists and propose good theories of suicide and conduct methodologically sound and important research on the topic. However, the 1980s have witnessed a swing of the pendulum toward the medical model of psychiatric illness, resulting in a slew of biochemical analyses of both completed and attempted suicides (see Lester, 1988).

The Goal of the Present Book

Since psychological theorists have not addressed the issue of suicide, the goal in the present book has been to take several of the major theorists and apply their ideas to suicide. Not every theorist has been included here because many of their theories have nothing to say about suicide. However, we have been able to take several major theorists, including Alfred Adler, Hans Eysenck, Sigmund Freud, George Kelly, Henry Murray, Carl Rogers, William Sheldon, and social learning theory, and explore their implications for suicide.

Leenaars (1988) in a provocative book has taken ten theorists and explored whether their views on suicide (or general psychological disturbance) explain the content of suicide notes. Some of the theorists Leenaars considered are included here (Freud, Kelly, Adler and Murray), but some are not, because their ideas have failed to generate any research on suicide (Binswanger, Jung and Sullivan), because their views are too similar to the classic theorists (Menninger and Zilborg), or because their views are not related to classic psychological theory (Shneidman).

Each chapter in the present book briefly presents the theory of human behavior proposed by the theorist, and discusses the specific way in which suicide is conceptualized in the theory and reviews research relevant to this conceptualization. The success of the theories will be examined in the concluding chapter, but here we may note that Freud's psychoanalytic theory, social learning theory and Eysenck's physiological theory each provide a rich framework for understanding suicide and for guiding future research.

REFERENCES

Bartlett, F.C.: *Remembering.* Cambridge: Cambridge University Press, 1932.

Durkheim, E.: *Suicide.* New York: Free Press, 1951.

Gibbs, J.P.: Testing the theory of status integration and suicide rates. *American Sociological Review,* 47:227-237, 1982.

Gibbs, J.P., & Martin, W.T.: *Status integration and suicide.* Eugene: University of Oregon Press, 1964.

Henry, A.F., & Short, J.F.: *Suicide and homicide.* New York: Free Press, 1954.

Leenaars, A.A.: *Suicide notes.* New York: Human Sciences Press, 1988.

Lester, D.: *The biochemical basis of suicide.* Springfield: Thomas, 1988.

Litman, R.E.: Sigmund Freud on Suicide. In E.S. Shneidman (Ed.) *Essays in self-destruction.* New York: Science House, 1967, 324-344.

Mehrabian, A., & Weinstein, L.: Temperament characteristics of suicide attempters. *Journal of Consulting & Clinical Psychology,* 53:544-546, 1985.

Pescosolido, B.A., & Mendelsohn, R.: Social causation or social construction. *American Sociological Review,* 51:80-101, 1986.

Persons, J.B.: The advantages of studying psychological phenomena rather than psychiatric diagnoses. *American Psychologist,* 1986, 41, 1252-1260.

Phillips, D.P.: The impact of fictional television stories on U.S. adult fatalities. *American Journal of Sociology,* 87:1340-1359, 1982.

Tomlinson-Keasey, C., Warren, L.W., & Elliott, J.E.: Suicide among gifted women. *Journal of Abnormal Psychology,* 95:123-130, 1985.

Turner, J.H., & Beeghley, L.: *The emergence of sociological theory.* Homewood: Dorsey, 1981.

Chapter 2

SIGMUND FREUD'S
PSYCHOANALYTIC THEORY

THE BASIC assumption made by Sigmund Freud was that all behavior is motivated.[1] The critical word here is "all." *All* behavior is
motivated, including our choice of career, our choice of a spouse, our
choice of clothes today, and even such trivial behaviors as tugging an
earlobe or stroking our nose as we read a book. This assumption is often
called the *principle of psychic determinism.*

Freud argued that each behavior was not determined simply by one
wish or motive, but probably by many. Furthermore, some of these
wishes are unconscious, so that we remain unaware of them and the fact
that they are determining our behavior.

Freud defined three major subsets of wishes. Id wishes are those that
we possess very early in life. They are simple, somewhat primitive and
unorganized, and often aggressive. When a small child says to his
parent, "I'm going to smash you with a cement truck," he is manifesting
an id wish. Id wishes rarely get satisfied directly, and many of them become unconscious as we grow up.

Superego wishes are wishes that we take over from other people,
chiefly our parents. They comprise two kinds: the prohibitions which
are commonly called our conscience ("Don't lie to your mother!" and
"You clean your plate or you'll not get any dessert!") and those wishes
that characterize what we would like to be, commonly called our ego-
ideal ("I want to be a lawyer when I grow up, just like my Daddy").

Ego wishes are complex, organized and mature wishes, best exempli-
fied by the kinds of wishes we show most of the time. Let us say we get

---

[1]The presentation of Freudian theory is based upon Toman (1960).

angry at our father because of something he does or says to us. An id wish might be that you would like to hit him and really hurt him. A superego wish might be that we should love our parents and it is wrong to hit them, and Daddy, upon whom you have modelled yourself, never hits people. An ego wish might be that you love your father, despite difficulties you have in relating to him; you feel a good deal of affection for him. The compromise is that you feel some anger, and eventually you write him a letter telling him how mad he made you. This behavior is motivated by, and a compromise of, all of these wishes (and probably many more that derive from your particular life situation).

The terms id, superego, and ego are best thought of as adjectives, and not as little structures inside your skull. But psychoanalysts easily slip into using the terms as nouns.

Development permits us to gain control over our wishes. We form derivative desires, which derive from the desires we had as infants and children. The desire to suck at your mother's breast leads to desires to suck at a bottle, a pacifier and thumb, candy, cigarettes and pipes, the end of your pencil as you read this book, to touch your lips with your finger when you think, to kiss the person you love, and so on. The early desire to drink your mother's milk has now developed into a liking for several hundred types of food and drink.

These derivative desires give you control because, if you have to give up one object of a desire, say lobster newburg, you have many other objects to take its place. A baby has few alternatives. Often it will not drink strange fluids.

In addition, as you grow up, you gain control over the conditions for gratifying desires. For example, you can feed yourself and prepare your own foods. The baby has to rely on mother.

The central concept for Freud was anxiety. Anxiety is generated in two ways. First, you become anxious whenever any wish of yours (conscious or unconscious) is deprived. Second, you become anxious whenever an unconscious wish is likely to become conscious to you.

Let us say you have an unconscious desire to attack your father. If you deprive that desire, you will become anxious. However, if you do anything that may make you aware of the desire, you will also become anxious. The solution is to satisfy it partially without realizing what you are really doing. You may turn the anger inward upon yourself and feel only depression, but no anger. Or you may meet someone that is like your father in some respects and get into a fight with him without noticing the similarity; for example, your employer or a guy in a bar. Or you may decide that your father hates you (rather than you hating him), and you avoid him.

The defense mechanisms describe these alternatives. In displacement, you argue with your employer. In reaction formation you deny that you hate your father but rather claim that you love him. In projection you decide that he hates you. And there are many more defense mechanisms that have been described.

All psychiatric symptoms and all abnormal behavior (as well as most normal behavior) are ways out of this dilemma — how to satisfy unconscious desires without becoming conscious of them. This leads to the critical psychoanalytic question — "I wonder what the *real* reason is for this person to have done that?" The superficially apparent answer is rarely the complete answer.

Freud also felt that deprivation of desires in early life had far-reaching implications later in life. The earlier that particular desires were deprived and the more severe the deprivation, the more severe the later psychological disturbance. Loss of a mother, for example, is more severe than loss of a father, and loss of a mother at age two is a more severe loss than loss at age four.

Freud on Suicide

Freud never considered the psychodynamics underlying suicidal behavior to any great extent. Brief mentions of suicidal behavior can be found throughout his writings, however, and Litman (1967) has attempted to document and synthesize these dispersed thoughts.

By 1910 Freud had recognized many clinical features of suicidal behavior: guilt over death wishes toward others, identification with a suicidal parent, refusal to accept loss of gratification, suicide as an act of revenge, suicide as an escape from humiliation, suicide as a communication, and the connection between death and sexuality.

The more systematic views began with his discussion of melancholia. The essential feature of suicidal behavior is that the person loses a loved object, and the energy withdrawn from this lost loved object is relocated in the ego and used to recreate the loved one as a permanent feature of the self, an identification of the ego with the lost object. Litman called this process ego-splitting.

Freud's formulation here is, of course, phrased in the more archaic version of his theory. In more modern terms, the person has already introjected some of the desires of the loved one. Children introject desires of their parents, and adults introject the desires of their lovers. In this way, it is as if part of your mind is also symbolic of your loved ones. Once this person is lost (by death or divorce, for example), we still possess those introjected desires, and thus the lost loved one remains symbolically as part of our own mind.

This process can lead to suicide when the person also harbors hostile wishes toward the lost object for now we can turn this anger toward that part of our mind which is modelled upon and symbolizes the lost object.

(More recently, Draper [1976] has suggested that attachment to the mother in the late oral stage is critical for the development of later suicidal behavior. If loss occurs during this phase, later losses cause regression to the loss of this first relationship. Suicide is then a relief from abandonment. People who never achieve this object differentiation and cathexis [such as schizophrenics] are less likely to complete suicide. Research has failed to support Draper's ideas, however, as we shall see later, since the age at the time of loss has not been found to be a significant factor in suicidal behavior.)

A later development in Freud's thought was the postulate of the existence of a death instinct, an instinctual drive toward death that is balanced by the life instinct. The death instinct is primarily masochistic and the individual tries to externalize the instinct as aggression or sadism. However, when there are cultural forces opposing sadism, the instinct is turned back onto the self. Futterman (1961) stressed that neither the life instinct nor the death instinct could really function independently of each other, but that they were always fused in variable amounts. Futterman suggested that it was reasonable to assume that both instincts went through a similar sequence of development during the psychological stages of development.

Litman pointed out that this later development moves to a very general level of discourse and focusses on the universal elements of man's lot. Thus, it is not clear how such a process can explain why some people kill themselves whereas others do not. At best, it provides a mere restatement of this fact. The earlier formulation was more heuristic in that it did propose a developmental process leading to suicide.

Freud's postulate of a death instinct can also be seen as a product of his era. Early in this Century, every psychological theorist felt the need to explain why humans behaved at all. Therefore, they all proposed energy concepts in their theories. After Hebb's (1949) classic book, *The Organization of Behavior*, psychological theorists no longer felt it necessary to explain why humans behaved. Rather, the motivational question focussed on why humans do *this* rather than *that*.

Tabachnick and Klugman (1967) have speculated on how the existence of a death instinct might be validated. Freud's energy concepts were based on the notion that the amount of energy in each person was a constant. We are born with a given level of libido/destrudo (the energies fueling the life and death instincts), and no matter how fast we expend these energies we are left with the same amount. In Toman's (1960) rational version of the theory, these energies are replaced by the concept of a rate of cathexis which remains constant for each individual over his life.

Tabachnick and Klugman argued that the death equivalent rate in the community, that is, the rate with which the death instinct is manifested, would be constant. Thus, if one manifestation of the death instinct is reduced, then other manifestations of the death instinct should be increased.

The problem here, of course, is deriving an exhaustive list of behaviors motivated by the death instinct. Suicide is clearly one. Tabachnick and Klugman suggested also certain kinds of accidents, psychosomatic illnesses, substance abuse, and self-destructive vocations and avocations. If rates of one or more of these go down, do the other rates go up? Tabachnick and Klugman did not present empirical data on their hypothesis.

Freud's hypothesis of a death instinct, untestable though it might be, had a great influence on thinking about suicide. For example, Menninger (1938) suggested that suicidal motivation can be seen behind behaviors which at first glance are not obviously suicidal. Menninger noted that some people shorten their lives by choosing self-destructive life styles, such as alcohol or drug abuse, heavy cigarette smoking, and so on. He called such behaviors *chronic suicide*. He also noted that some people appear to focus their self-destructive impulses on specific parts of their bodies, leaving their mind unimpaired. For example, a person may blind himself or lose an arm in an industrial accident. Menninger saw the death instinct as behind such behaviors, and he called them *focal suicide*.

The result of this has been some interest on the part of suicidologists in indirect self-destructive behavior, as in Farberow's (1980) edited collection of papers, and on life-threatening behavior in general. The official journal of the American Association of Suicidology is called *Suicide and Life-Threatening Behavior*.

Of course, other writers on suicide have objected to this broadening of the term *suicide*. Goldstein (1940), for example, would restrict the use of the word suicide to behaviors with a conscious intent to kill the person, who must have a mature concept of death.

The Real Reasons for Suicide

One major influence of psychoanalytic theory on the analysis of suicides is the asking of the question: what is the *real* reason for this suicide? Typically, investigators listed (and still do list) the most common precipitating events for suicides, and the lists typically include break-up of a close relationship, financial problems, legal problems, and so on.

The problem with this is that the vast majority of those in our society who have these experiences do not kill themselves. These precipitating events are neither necessary nor sufficient to account for suicide. This led psychoanalysts to probe for the psychological and possibly unconscious motives behind the suicidal act.

Of course, each suicide has his own unique motives. For example, the suicide of Sylvia Plath seems to be clearly in part Oedipal in nature based on her own writings. In the poem *Daddy*, she expresses affection and anger toward her deceased father, describes her marriage as an attempt to find a father substitute, and casts her suicide as a reunion with daddy.

However, some writers have identified general motives. For example, Menninger (1938) suggested three motives for suicide: the desire to die (to escape from unbearable psychological or physical pain), the desire to kill (where the person is angry and aggressing toward others), and the desire to be killed (where the person feels guilty and depressed and is aggressing toward himself). Hendin (1965) has speculated on the different psychodynamics for suicide in the three Scandinavian countries.

The Frustration-Aggression Hypothesis

The frustration-aggression hypothesis developed by Dollard, et al. (1939) proposed that aggression is often a consequence of frustration. Henry and Short (1954) took this idea and proposed that the basic and primary aggressive response to frustration is to aggress against the frustrating person rather than the self. They then attempted to search for constraints that would legitimate or inhibit this other-oriented aggression. What enables a child to develop so that his primary response to frustration, that of other-oriented aggression, is seen as legitimate, while other children develop in such a way that this primary response is inhibited and self-directed aggression becomes legitimate?

They focussed first on the existence of external constraints in the society. If there are strong external constraints in the society, then other-directed aggression stays legitimized. When behavior is required to conform rigidly to the demands and expectations of others, the share of others in the responsibility for the consequences of the behavior increases, legitimizing the other-oriented aggression. When external constraints are weak, the self must bear the responsibility for the frustration generated, and other-oriented aggression fails to be legitimized.

At the psychological level, Henry and Short focussed on experiences of childhood punishment. They argued that love-oriented punishment and punishment by the parent who is the major source of nurturance in the family will lead to the inhibition of other-oriented aggression (toward the punishing parent) because to aggress against him or her would threaten the supply of love and nurturance. In contrast, physical punishment and punishment by the parent who is not the major source of nurturance and love would not inhibit the other-directed aggressive response to punishment since to aggress against the punishing parent would be less likely to threaten the supply of love and nurturance.

The frustration-aggression hypothesis applied to suicide is clearly related to the psychoanalytic approach.

Leenaars's Research on Suicide Notes

Leenaars (1988) has summarized Freud's views on the suicidal individual in ten propositions:

1. Though the person has conscious desires to kill himself, the act appears also to be motivated by unconscious desires.
2. The suicidal person is preoccupied with a person who he has lost or who has rejected him.
3. He feels ambivalent about the lost or rejecting person, that is, both affectionate and hostile.
4. He is in some direct or indirect fashion identifying himself with the rejecting or lost person.
5. He appears to be treating himself as if he were reacting to another person.
6. The person has feelings of vengefullness and aggression toward himself as well as anger toward others.
7. The person is turning back upon himself murderous impulses felt toward some other person.
8. The person sees his suicide as a way of punishing himself.
9. The person feels guilt and is self-critical.
10. The person feels that his personal organization of his experiences is impaired, and he can no longer synthesize his experiences properly.

Leenaars found that these ten ideas were found more often in a sample of genuine suicide notes than in a sample of simulated notes. In particular, statements 2, 3, 6, 7, and 8 were found more often in genuine notes. However, none of the statements were found to be present in at least two-thirds of the genuine notes.

Research Related to Psychoanalytic Hypotheses

Experience of Loss

Many studies have been conducted on whether suicidal individuals have had more experience of loss in their early years. Lester (1972) reviewed research from the 1960s and earlier while Lester (1983) reviewed research from the 1970s.

In the 1970s, twelve studies reported no excess of childhood loss of parents in suicidal individuals while thirteen studies reported an excess of childhood loss. Interestingly, no studies found less experience of loss in suicidal individuals.

Overall, the age at loss and the sex of the parent lost appeared to be unrelated to being suicidal. Phillips (1979), in his review of the same literature, felt that loss due to separation or divorce (but not death) might be more common in both completed and attempted suicides, that loss might be more common in younger suicidal individuals, and that loss of a parent by death might be associated with more severe suicidal actions.

Bunch (1972; Bunch, et. al., 1971) has reported an excess of recent loss of parents in some completed suicides (mainly in those younger, single and male) and an excess of recent loss of a spouse. Kearney (1970) found an excess of early loss of parents due to separation and divorce and an excess of recent disruptions in interpersonal relationships in a sample of attempted suicides. Stein, et al. (1974) reported an excess of both early and later loss in suicide attempters.

Lester and Beck (1976) explored this further and reported that female suicide attempters who had experienced early childhood separation from parents were more likely to have a recent loss as a precipitant for their suicide attempt. (This was not found for males.) Lester and Beck concluded that early loss may sensitize the individual to later loss, and this hypothesis merits further examination.

Suicide and Depression

In psychoanalytic theory, suicide is seen as an extreme form of depression, in which anger is turned inward upon the self. There is good evidence that suicide is strongly associated with depression. Suicide rates are commonly found to be highest in psychiatric patients with a diagnosis of depression (for example, Temoche, et al., 1964). Whereas about one percent of the deaths of the general population are from suicide, about fifteen percent of patients with affective disorders die from suicide (Guze and Robins, 1970).

Beck and his associates have conducted several studies showing that depression (and especially its cognitive component, hopelessness) were powerful predictors of suicide (for example, Beck, et al., 1975). Lester, et al. (1979) showed that those attempted suicides who later completed suicide were among the most depressed and hopeless patients during their initial suicide attempt.

Thus, suicide is strongly associated with depression as expected from the perspective of psychoanalytic theory.

Suicide and Aggression

Psychoanalytic theory leads to the prediction that suicidal people should have inhibited their aggression and turned it inward upon themselves. Thus, they should be relatively nonaggressive.

Several psychiatric studies have noted that suicidal individuals are more likely to have temper tantrums (Offenkrantz, et al., 1957), report hostility and anger (Braaten and Darling, 1962; Wolff, 1971; Conte and Plutchik, 1974), engage in crimes against people and property (Marjot, 1966; Myers and Neal, 1978), assault others in the psychiatric hospital (Farberow, et al., 1966; Kangas and Mahrer, 1970; Sletten, et al., 1973), have been in more fights and brawls (Whitlock and Broadhurst, 1969), and use verbal and physical aggression in family arguments (Pomeroy, et al., 1965).

Kinsinger (1973) and Lester (1967, 1968) found that suicidal people had as high levels of direct, verbal and indirect aggression as nonsuicidal college students. Both McEvoy (1963) and Vogel (1968) found that suicidal psychiatric patients made up as aggressive stories as did nonsuicidal patients. On the Rosenzweig Picture-Frustration Test, no consistent differences have been identified between suicidal and nonsuicidal individuals (Lester, 1970). Philip (1970) found that attempted suicides obtained as high general hostility scores as nonsuicidal people.

Raphling (1970) found that suicidal people had more aggressive dreams than nonsuicidal patients. On the other hand, Spiegel, et al. (1969) found that suicidal patients preferred intropunitive jokes more

than did nonsuicidal patients. Thurber and Torbet (1978) found that suicidal individuals preferred aggressive words less than nonsuicidal individuals.

The results of these studies show two trends. First, in clinical studies,
suicidal people are often found to be among the most aggressive and
violent patients. In studies using psychological tests, suicidal individuals
are found to be similar in anger and aggression to nonsuicidal individuals. Only two studies out of this body of research suggested that suicidal people might be less aggressive, and those studies studied word and
joke preferences. Thus, on the whole, the research on aggression in suicidal individuals does not support the hypothesis that they inhibit aggression in general.

It should be noted, however, that this research has been conducted on
attempted suicides or those with suicidal ideation. It may well be that
completed suicides do show a pattern of inhibiting outward-directed anger
and turn it inward on the self.

Punishment Experiences

Very little research has been conducted on the punishment experiences of suicidal individuals. Gold (1958) found that some groups who
would be expected to have experience of physical punishment (such as
males and enlistees in the military) would have lower suicide rates than
other groups (such as females and officers respectively). Lester (1967a)
tested these ideas using a sample of nonliterate societies with ratings
available for both suicide and homicide rates and the use of different
techniques of punishment. He found no associations.

Lester (1968a) explored the recollections of suicidal and nonsuicidal
students about their childhood experiences of punishment and found no
differences.

Much more research needs to be conducted on this important issue.

Are Suicide and Homicide Polar Opposites?

Lester (1987) reviewed research relevant to the notion that suicide
and homicide are alternative ways of directing aggression. Research on
whether suicidal people are nonaggressive was reviewed above, where it
was concluded that there was no evidence that suicidal individuals are
less outwardly aggressive than nonsuicidal individuals. Some of the research showed that they were as aggressive as nonsuicidal people, while
other research showed that they were more aggressive. Lester noted that

no study had combined the elements of directing aggression inwards *and* loss of a loved object.

Surprisingly, very few studies have compared suicides with murderers. Pokorny (1965) compared attempted suicides, completed suicides, murderers and assaulters, but used simple sociodemographic variables and the circumstances of the act. Murderers resembled assaulters closely. Murderers and completed suicides differed greatly. Attempted suicides resembled the suicides in some variables and the murderers in others.

In a series of Rorschach studies, Lester (Lester, et al., 1974, 1975; Lester and Perdue, 1974) found that Rorschach signs developed to pick-out suicides also identified murderers. Furthermore, signs to differentiate murderers from nonviolent criminals classified completed suicides as murderers.

Thus, there is little evidence that suicides and murderers differ in personality, but they do seem to differ in sociodemographic characteristics. In Pokorny's research, the murderers were more often black and young while the suicides were more often white and old. However, more psychological comparisons of suicides and murderers need to be carried out to clarify the similarities and differences.

Large numbers of sociological studies of the relationship between suicide rates and homicide rates and between these rates of personal violence and other sociological variables have been conducted. These correlations have been carried out over regions, time, and sociological subgroups within a society. Lester (1987) reviewed eight of his own studies using a limited sample of eighteen industrialized nations and found that the suicide and murder rates were not related in opposite ways to sociological variables. For example, while the quality of life was related to murder rates, it was not related to suicide rates. On the other hand, the proportion of people with different blood types was related to suicide rates but not to homicide rates.

However, these results are quite different if a sample of nations with a greater diversity of economic development is included. Then, homicide and suicide rates do seem to be polar opposites. For example, in a sample of forty-three nations, Lester (1984) found that suicide rates were related positively while homicide rates were related negatively to the quality of life.

These methodological problems make it difficult to give a simple answer to the question of whether suicide and homicide are polar opposites from a societal perspective. However, the question has value as a stimulant for research.

Frustration and Suicide

Although research into suicide has studied the effects of loss and stress, little research has focussed on frustration. The only studies directly pertinent to frustration were conducted by Naroll. Naroll (1965) found that nonliterate societies with a high incidence of frustration (or thwarting disorientation to use Naroll's terminology) were also those with a high rate of suicide. Krauss and Krauss (1968) examined individual cases of suicide and found that societies with a high incidence of frustrating situations (such as wife-beating, marriage restrictions, drunken brawling, frequent warfare, and so on) had a high rate of suicide that took place in a social context of thwarting disorientation, but no higher incidence of other types of suicide.

It would be of great interest to develop measures of both the subjective experience of frustration and of a history of frustrations experienced and to explore whether such measures bear any relationship to the experience of suicide.

Conclusions

It can be seen that psychoanalytic theory has greatly influenced the kinds of questions that we ask about suicide, as indeed it has influenced the kinds of questions we ask about people's behavior in general.

In addition, a large amount of research into suicide has been stimulated by psychoanalytic theory or is relevant to the theory. Suicidal people do seem to have experienced much loss in childhood which may sensitize them to later loss. Suicide is strongly associated with depression, while not apparently associated with a general inhibition of anger and aggressive behavior.

It is evident that psychoanalytic theory can prove useful in furthering our understanding of suicidal behavior.

REFERENCES

Beck, A., Kovacs, M., & Weissman, A.: Hopelessness and suicidal behavior. *Journal of the American Medical Association*, 234:1146-1149, 1975.

Braaten, L., & Darling, C.: Suicidal tendencies among college students. *Psychiatric Quarterly*, 36:665-692, 1962.

Bunch, J.: Recent bereavement in relation to suicide. *Journal of Psychosomatic Research*, 16:361-366, 1972.

Bunch, J., Barraclough, B., Nelson, B., & Sainsbury, P.: Early parental bereavement and suicide. *Social Psychiatry*, 6:200-202, 1971.

Conte, H., & Plutchik, R.: Personality and background characteristics of suicidal mental patients. *Journal of Psychiatric Research*, 10:181-188, 1974.

Dollard, J., Doob, L., Miller, N., Mowrer, O., & Sears, R.: *Frustration and aggression.* New Haven: Yale University Press, 1938.

Draper, E.: A developmental theory of suicide. *Comprehensive Psychiatry*, 17:63-80, 1976.

Farberow, N.: *The many faces of suicide.* New York: McGraw-Hill, 1980.

Farberow, N., Shneidman, E., & Neuringer, C.: Case history and hospitalization factors in suicides of neuropsychiatric hospital patients. *Journal of Nervous & Mental Diseases*, 142:32-44, 1966.

Futterman, S.: Suicide. In N. Farberow & E. Shneidman (Eds.) *The cry for help.* New York: McGraw-Hill, 1961, 167-180.

Gold, M.: Suicide, homicide and the socialization of aggression. *American Journal of Sociology*, 63:651-661, 1958.

Goldstein, K.: *Human nature in the light of psychopathology.* Cambridge: Harvard University Press, 1940.

Guze, S., & Robins, E.: Suicide and primary affective disorders. *British Journal of Psychiatry*, 117:437-438, 1970.

Hebb, D.: *The organization of behavior.* New York: 1949.

Hendin, H.: *Suicide and Scandinavia.* New York: Doubleday, 1965.

Henry, A., & Short, J.: *Suicide and homicide.* Glencoe: Free Press, 1954.

Kangas, P., & Mahrer, A.: Suicide attempts and threats as goal-directed communications in psychotic males. *Psychological Reports*, 27:795-801, 1970.

Kearney, T.: Aetiology of attempted suicide. *Proceedings of the 5th International Congress for Suicide Prevention.* Vienna: IASP, 1970, 190-194.

Kinsinger, J.: Women who threaten suicide. *Omega*, 4:73-84, 1973.

Krauss, H., & Krauss, B.: Cross-cultural study of the thwarting-disorientation theory of suicide. *Journal of Abnormal Psychology*, 73:353-357, 1968.

Leenaars, A.A.: *Suicide notes.* New York: Human Sciences Press, 1988.

Lester, D.: Suicide as an aggressive act. *Journal of Psychology*, 66:47-50, 1967.

Lester, D.: Suicide, homicide and the effects of socialization. *Journal of Personality & Social Psychology*, 5:466-468, 1967a.

Lester, D.: Suicide as an aggressive act. *Journal of General Psychology*, 79:83-86, 1968.

Lester, D.: Punishment experiences and suicidal preoccupation. *Journal of Genetic Psychology*, 113:89-94, 1968a.

Lester, D.: Attempts to predict suicidal risk using psychological tests. *Psychological Bulletin*, 74:1017, 1970.

Lester, D.: *Why people kill themselves.* Springfield: Thomas, 1972.

Lester, D.: *Why people kill themselves.* Springfield: Thomas, 1983.

Lester, D.: The association between the quality of life and suicide and homicide rates. *Journal of Social Psychology*, 124:247-248, 1984.

Lester, D.: Murders and suicide. *Behavioral Sciences & the Law*, 49-60, 1987.

Lester, D., & Beck, A.: Early loss as a possible sensitizer to later loss in attempted suicides. *Psychological Reports*, 39:121-122, 1976.

Lester, D., Beck, A., & Mitchell, B.: Extrapolation from attempted suicide to completed suicide. *Journal of Abnormal Psychology*, 88:78-80, 1979.

Lester, D., Kendra, J., & Perdue, W.: Distinguishing murderers from suicides with the Rorschach. *Perceptual & Motor Skills*, 39:474, 1974.

Lester, D., Kendra, J., Thisted, R., & Perdue, W.: Prediction of homicide with the Rorschach. *Journal of Clinical Psychology*, 31:752, 1975.

Lester, D., & Perdue, W.: The detection of attempted suicides and murderers using the Rorschach. *Journal of Psychiatric Research*, 10:101-103, 1974.

Litman, R.: Sigmund Freud on suicide. In E. Shneidman (Ed.) *Essays in self-destruction*. New York: Science House, 1967, 324-344.

Marjot, D.: Aggressive psychopathology. *Journal of the Royal Navy Medical Service*, 52:71-77, 1966.

McEvoy, T.: A comparison of suicidal and nonsuicidal patients by means of the TAT. *Dissertation Abstracts*, 24:1248, 1963.

Menninger, K.: *Man against himself*. New York: Harcourt Brace & World, 1938.

Myers, D., & Neal, C.: Suicide in psychiatric patients. *British Journal of Psychiatry*, 133:38-44, 1978.

Naroll, R.: Thwarting disorientation and suicide. Unpublished, Northwestern University, 1965.

Offenkrantz, W., Church, E., & Elliott, R.: Psychiatric management of suicide problems in military service. *American Journal of Psychiatry*, 114:33-41, 1957.

Philip, A.: Personality characteristics of attempted suicides in Edinburgh. *Proceedings of the 5th International Congress for Suicide Prevention*. Vienna: IASP, 1970, 114-116.

Phillips, D.: A review of incidence of parental absence upon suicidal behavior. *Proceedings of the 10th International Congress for Suicide Prevention*. Ottawa: IASP, 1979, 50-53.

Pokorny, A.: Human violence. *Journal of Criminal Law, Criminology & Police Science*, 56:488-497, 1965.

Pomeroy, E., Mahrer, A., & Mason, D.: An aggressive syndrome in hospitalized patients. *Proceedings of the American Psychological Association*, 239-240, 1965.

Raphling, D.: Dreams and suicide attempts. *Journal of Nervous & Mental Disease*, 151:404-410, 1970.

Sletten, I., Evenson, R., & Brown, M.: Some results from an automated statewide comparison among attempted, committed and nonsuicidal patients. *Life-Threatening Behavior*, 3:191-197, 1973.

Spiegel, D., Keith-Spiegel, P., Abrahams, J., & Kranitz, L.: Humor and suicide. *Journal of Consulting & Clinical Psychology*, 33:504-505, 1969.

Stein, M., Levy, M., & Glasberg, M.: Separations in black and white suicide attempters. *Archives of General Psychiatry*, 31:815-821, 1974.

Tabachnick, N., & Klugman, D.: Suicide research and the death instinct. *Yale Scientific Magazine*, 6:12-15, 1967.

Temoche, A., Pugh, T., & MacMahon, B.: Suicide rates among current and former mental institution patients. *Journal of Nervous & Mental Diseases*, 138:124-130, 1964.

Thurber, S., & Torbet, D.: On the word preferences of suicidal versus nonsuicidal college students. *Journal of Consulting & Clinical Psychology*, 46:362-363, 1978.

Toman, W.: *An introduction to the psychoanalytic theory of motivation.* New York: Pergamon, 1960.

Vogel, R.: A projective study of dynamic factors in attempted suicide. *Dissertation Abstracts,* 28B:4303-4304, 1968.

Whitlock, F., & Broadhurst, A.: Attempted suicide and the experience of violence. *Journal of Biosocial Science,* 1:353-368, 1969.

Wolff, K.: The treatment of the depressed and suicidal geriatric patient. *Geriatrics,* 26(7):65-69, 1971.

Chapter 3

LEARNING AND
SOCIAL LEARNING THEORY

THE LEARNING theory of human behavior uses the same learning paradigms that have been identified by psychologists who ex-
perimented with lower animals in laboratory research. It is assumed that
these paradigms are appropriately applicable to humans, and that humans learn behaviors in the same way as these lower animals learn.

Two major learning paradigms have been identified over the years.
First, in *classical conditioning*, previously neutral stimuli (the conditioned
stimuli) become associated with other stimuli (the unconditioned stimuli) that produce responses. Eventually, after many pairings, the formerly neutral stimuli now elicit the response.

To take an example, erotic pornography elicits sexual arousal in normal heterosexual males. Rachman and Hodgson (1968) paired pictures of
boots with the erotic pornography, and eventually the boots elicited sexual
arousal. The boots (the conditioned stimulus) now elicit the response that
formerly only erotic pornography (the unconditioned stimulus) elicited.
Rachman had produced a (temporary) fetish in these males.

Punishment functions by means of classical conditioning. The punishing unconditioned stimulus produces unconditioned responses, such as
fear and pain, which by classical conditioning become attached to the
formerly neutral stimuli, the misbehavior of which the punisher disap-
proves.

If the teacher omits the unconditioned stimulus, eventually the conditioned response to the conditioned stimulus disappears, or *extinguishes*.
After extinction, the conditioned stimulus again becomes neutral.

The second major learning paradigm is operant conditioning. In
operant conditioning, if a response is made in the presence of a stimulus

and is followed by a reinforcer (or reward), then the response is more likely to be emitted in the presence of the stimulus in the future. Reinforcers are of two kinds. Positive reinforcers are the onset of something nice whereas negative reinforcers are the ending of something nasty.

To take an example here, our baby is left alone in his crib, and the light turned out as his mother leaves his bedroom. He cries and, after a while, his mother returns and turns the light on to see if he is all right. The response of crying has been rewarded, both by the positive reinforcer of his mother's presence and attention, but also by the negative reinforcer of the ending of darkness and of being alone. His mother is teaching him to cry at night.

Operant conditioning can be used to *shape* a new behavior. Initially, the person is rewarded for approximations to the response that the teacher wants. As the person begins to offer these approximations to the desired behavior, the teacher enforces a stricter criterion before rewarding responses. This is the way, for example, that children acquire competent speech.

The schedule of reinforcement has been found to be an important determinant of the strength of learning. Partial reinforcement schedules (in which the person is rewarded for only some responses to the stimulus) have been found to lead to stronger learning than continuous reinforcement schedules.

In *generalization*, the person who is trained to respond to one particular stimulus generalizes this response to other similar stimuli. However, if the person is not rewarded for responding to these similar stimuli, he eventually ceases to respond to them and has learned *discrimination*.

Social Learning Theory

Social learning theory (Bandura, 1977) modified simple learning theory by taking into account the fact that humans have thoughts, beliefs and expectations which can affect the simple learning paradigms described above. Thoughts can provide stimuli, responses can be imagined and reinforcers can be cognitions (such as self-praise).

Thus, for example, a person can engage in trial-and-error, problem-solving tasks using solely internal thoughts, so that an observer would observe no stimuli, responses, or reinforcers. Social learning theory also accepts too that humans can learn by watching others (by modeling or imitation).

Bandura also introduced the concept of *self-efficacy*. This is the belief that you can have an impact on your life-space. People can believe that their actions would result in certain outcomes if they performed these actions—outcome expectations. They can also believe that they can bring about a particular outcome—efficacy expectation.

Efficacy expectations are formed by the person's history of successes and failures, vicarious experiences (by watching others perform tasks), and by a variety of other life experiences.

Learning Theories of Depression

Two major learning theories of depression have been proposed.

Inadequate Reinforcement

Lewinsohn (1974) has argued that depression is caused by a lack of reinforcement. For example, responses that were rewarded in the past are no longer rewarded because the source of the rewards is no longer present. A spouse may have died, children may have moved away, or a job may have been lost through being laid-off or through retirement. Without these positive reinforcers, the person no longer performs the responses that were formerly rewarded. The person, therefore, becomes passive and withdrawn.

Lewinsohn noted that the amount of reinforcement that a person receives is determined by the number of events that a person finds reinforcing, the availability of the reinforcements in the environment, and the ability to emit the behaviors that will elicit the reinforcers. The person may lose rewards through any of these three possibilities.

In support of this theory, Lewinsohn found that, if depressed people are placed in highly rewarding situations, then their mood improves, that a person's mood was associated with the number of rewards he was receiving (Lewinsohn and Graf, 1973), and also that depressed patients possessed fewer social skills than nondepressed people.

Ferster (1974), too, has conceptualized depressed people as those who fail to stay in effective contact with the rewards of their environment and who fail to avoid its aversive aspects. In particular, depressed people are failing to obtain adequate amounts of reinforcement.

Learned Helplessness

Seligman (1974) argued that depression was a manifestation of a phenomenon that he called learned helplessness. Seligman exposed dogs to inescapable electric shock. When he then permitted these dogs to escape the painful electric shocks, they did not learn to do so. In contrast, dogs not previously exposed to the inescapable electric shock soon learned to escape the electric shocks. Seligman suggested that the dogs who were forced to endure inescapable electric shock had learned to be helpless, that is, they had learned that the shock was always inescapable. The experience of previous failure caused them to make little effort in the future.

In human depression, therefore, it has been argued that, in psychologically painful situations, the person tried to escape the pain, but failed. He then generalized from this experience and learned (or decided) that he could never escape the pain.

We might note that this learning process may be especially potent if the person engages in cognitive distortions of the kind described by Albert Ellis (1973) and David Burns (1980). For example, if after the loss of a lover, the person says to himself, "I'll *never* find someone who will love me. I will *always* be alone," then he will be much more likely to show learned helplessness behavior in the future.

These ideas are clearly tied to the popular personality trait of belief in locus of control (Rotter, 1966). Rotter described three beliefs about who controls the outcomes of our life. We may believe that what happens to us is a function primarily of what we do, our actions. (I failed this exam because I did not study hard enough.) This is a belief in an internal locus of control. Alternatively, we may believe that what happens to us is a function of how powerful others respond to us. (That professor never liked me. I bet he graded me more harshly than the others.) And finally, we may believe that luck and fate determines the outcomes in our life. (It just wasn't my day to take an exam. My horoscope said so that morning.) These latter two beliefs are called belief in an external locus of control.

It would seem that those who believe in an external locus of control would be more susceptible to learned helplessness and also depression caused by learned helplessness. But the situation may be more complex than that. Henry and Short (1954) have argued that as long as we can blame someone else for our misfortunes, then outwardly expressed anger becomes legitimized. On the other hand, if we have only ourselves to blame for our misfortunes, then outwardly expressed anger is no longer legitimate, and we will be depressed and suicidal.

Lester (1983) reviewed the research on belief in locus of control and suicidal involvement. Three studies found that suicidal people had a stronger belief in an external locus of control: Henderson (1972) in college students, Levenson (1973) in serious suicide attempters, and Budner and Kumler (1973) in those thinking of suicide. However, three studies found no differences in belief in locus of control between suicidal and nonsuicidal people (Henderson, 1972 [in psychiatric patients];

Robins, et al., 1977; Lambley and Silbowitz, 1973). However, Lester found no study showing that suicidal people were more likely to have a belief in an internal locus of control, so this research does support the learned helplessness theory of depression for suicidal people.

In addition, Seligman noted that depressed people typically decide that the cause of their failure is stable and will persist into the future. Thus, they see their depressed state as permanent rather than transient. They may label themselves as stupid or the task as too difficult (an internal and an external factor respectively). Both of these causes are stable.

Finally, depressed people generalize from their failures. Rather than seeing their failure as specific to that particular task in that situation at that time, they anticipate a continued progression of failures in all kinds of situations in the future.

Depression as a Rewarded Behavior

Frederick and Resnick (1971) noted that depression may be rewarded by significant others. Depressed behaviors may elicit positive reinforcers from others such as care-taking behaviors, the so-called secondary gain.

Furthermore, parents may actually punish the child for aggressive responses, thereby facilitating the inhibition of the outward expression of anger. This blocked anger may then be turned inward onto the self and manifest itself as depression, the traditional psychoanalytic view of depression.

Cognitive and Rational Therapies

The cognitive and rational therapies focus on the ways that people think and their problem solving skills. Those who suffer from psychological problems typically are found to think irrationally and irresponsibly and to have very poor problem solving skills.

Rational-emotive therapy, devised by Ellis (1973), is concerned with emotions that impair our existence. Let us say that the client experiences some unpleasant experience, a failure or a rejection. This is the *activating experience*. In the unhealthy sequence, there follows an irrational belief. "Isn't it awful that she rejected me? I am worthless. No desirable woman will ever accept me. I deserve to be punished for my ineptness." Next, particular emotional states result from this irrational belief. The patient feels anxiety, depression, worthlessness or hostility. This is the *consequence*.

In the healthy sequence, the activating experience is followed by a *rational belief.* "Isn't it unfortunate, annoying or a pity that she rejected me." And consequent on this rational belief are the emotional states of regret, disappointment and annoyance.

Rational beliefs increase happiness and minimize pain. They are related to observable, empirically valid events. Irrational beliefs decrease happiness and maximize pain. They are related to magical, empirically invalid hypotheses for which there is no evidence. They prevent the client from fulfilling his desires in the future.

Counseling involves teaching the client that his emotional states are not a result of the activating experiences, but rather the irrational beliefs. The client must be taught to dispute the irrational beliefs. Why is it awful? How am I worthless? Where is the evidence that no one will ever love me? Why should I have done a better job? By what law do I deserve to be punished? Once the client can substitute rational beliefs for his irrational beliefs, he will be much happier and make appropriate decisions.

Burns (1980) has listed some common irrational ways of thinking. In *all-or-nothing thinking*, you view things as black or white. A less than perfect performance is a failure. In *overgeneralization*, one negative event is seen as a never-ending pattern of defeat. In *mental filter*, you dwell on negative details and filter out the positive aspects, and in *disqualifying the positive* you re-label positive experiences as "not counting" for some reason or another. In *magnification* or *catastrophizing* you exaggerate the importance of something. (For example, you say "This is the worst thing that could have happened to me," when it is far from the worst thing.) You *label* yourself or others (which leads to overgeneralization). I am a jerk or a loser. You are a louse or an evil person. These labels are distortions, but serve to create irrational emotions. In *jumping to conclusions*, we read the mind of someone else without checking it with them. Or we predict the future outcome negatively and so do not bother to attempt the task. In *shoulding*, we try to motivate ourselves by saying "I must..." or "I ought..." and so feel guilty when we do not. (It is preferable to say "It would be nice if I...")

For example, a depressed person may engage in "fortune-telling." He may see an opportunity for pleasure, say a social interaction. But he may anticipate that the other person will reject his advances, and so he will not make the social contact. He anticipated the loss of reinforcement (or even the punishment) in his thinking.

In direct decision therapy, Greenwald (1973) focuses upon the decisions that people make. Greenwald sees the task of the therapist as helping clients make decisions to change their behavior and helping them carry out these decisions.

In order to do this, the therapist must focus on the decision making process of the client. The first question to ask a client who enters therapy is "What's your problem?" Specific situational problems are easier to focus upon. "I have an unhappy marriage," or "I am afraid of heights" sets out a clear problem. A characterological problem is less specific. For example, "I am depressed" or "I am passive" express a way of being and of living. However, Greenwald sees such characterological problems as decisions that the client made. People *choose* to be depressed or passive. The therapist has to search with the client for the past decision that started this life style. Greenwald also urges the importance of finding out about the context in which former decisions were made. Once the context is found, the decision will no longer appear to be irrational.

In helping people to change, Greenwald focusses on the payoffs of various decisions. This must be done without criticizing the client. The positive gain and the negative gain from the decisions that have been made must both be examined.

Then, the client must be confronted with the decision, "Would you like to change?" Greenwald is opposed to forcing clients to change. It is not for the therapist to decide this, but for the client. One way to help clients to decide this is to help them locate alternatives. Often, they are unable to spontaneously think up alternatives, but with the therapist's encouragement, they usually can. It is important that the client does most of this work himself. Greenwald wants people to learn a system by which they can solve future problems by themselves, and so it is important that they be active in therapy.

Once a client has chosen an alternative, he must be encouraged to look at the payoffs once again. These payoffs and consequences must be compared with the payoffs of the previous decision. Greenwald is content to have the client stop here. He wants the client to be *aware* of his choices. *He does not have to change.* However, if he does decide to change, the therapist can help him carry it through. The therapist has to make sure that the client realizes that a decision has to be re-affirmed constantly and that one lapse does not mean that he has to abandon his new decision.

For Greenwald, then, depression is a choice that a client makes. He chooses to be depressed, and he does so because the payoff (the positive gain minus the negative gain) is attractive. He does not change because other alternatives do not seem to offer as good a payoff or because he lacks the skills required for alternative choices.

Thus, depression in this perspective is a choice made on the basis of relatively simple operant conditioning principles. It is maintained on the basis of the rewards. But its genesis varies from client to client, and Greenwald offered no general principles to explain the genesis of the choice.

Depression and Suicide

Suicide appears to be strongly linked to depression. Although only about one percent of all deaths are due to suicide, Guze and Robins (1970) found that the proportion of deaths due to completed suicide for those diagnosed with affective disorders was 15 percent. (These deaths tend to occur sooner than deaths from other causes, so estimates based on short follow-ups tend to be higher.)

A few studies have calculated suicide rates for patients with various psychiatric diagnoses. Temoche, et al. (1964) found the standard mortality ratio (the number of suicides expected on the basis of age-specific suicide rates expressed as a percentage of the number of suicides observed) for those with depressive psychoses to be 3610. Patients with psychoneuroses had the next highest ratio, of only 1840. Pokorny (1964) found a suicide rate of 566 per 100,000 per year for male VA psychiatric patients as compared to a rate of only 165 for psychiatric patients in general.

Barraclough (1972) examined one hundred cases of suicide and found that 64 had depressive illnesses. Of these, 44 had previous depressive episodes, and 21 of these met a strict criterion for diagnosing "recurrent affective illness."

Depression is strongly associated with attempted suicide too. Achte and Lonnqvist (1970) reported that depressive diagnoses were more common in attempted suicides than in other psychiatric patients, while McHugh and Goodell (1971) found that attempted suicides diagnosed as having depressive disorders made more serious attempts than those diagnosed as having personality disorders. Mintz et al. (1979) found that male VA patients who had attempted suicide were more depressed than veterans in general or methadone patients. Pallis and Sainsbury (1976) found that attempters with high suicidal intent had more depressive symptoms than those with low suicidal intent.

Beck and his associates have explored the relationship between suicidal preoccupation and depression in depth. It appears that the cognitive components of depression are most strongly associated with suicidal tendencies. Beck has called this component hopelessness and has devised a special psychological test to measure it.

For example, Silver et al. (1971) found that attempted suicides were more depressed than psychiatric patients and that depression scores correlated with an objective measure of suicidal intent in the attempted suicides. Lester and Beck (1977) found that suicidal ideators were more depressed than suicide attempters. Among suicidal ideators, suicidal wishes were associated most strongly with the cognitive aspects of depression, and Beck and Lester (1973; Lester and Beck, 1975) found the same to be true for attempted suicides.

Minkoff et al. (1973) and Beck et al. (1975) found that hopelessness was a stronger correlate of suicidal intent than depression. Beck et al. (1979) found the same to be true for suicidal ideation. This same result was found for alcohol abusers in the sample of attempted suicides (Beck et al. 1976) and for drug abusers (Weissman et al. 1979).

Discussion

This section has introduced the learning model for abnormal behavior in general and then reviewed learning theories of depression in particular. It has been shown that there are two main learning theories of depression, and that the cognitive and rational therapies provide a more complex social learning theory of depression. Since depression is strongly associated with suicidal behavior, a learning theory of depression goes far toward explaining suicide.

Learning Self-Injurious Behavior and Suicide: Manipulative Aspects

Self-injurious behavior is where a person harms, damages or mutilates himself (Lester, 1972b). The individual may bite or scratch himself, bang his head, or punch himself, occasionally producing severe physical damage. Carr (1977) and deCatanzaro (1981) have reviewed theories of the etiology of self-injurious behavior in retarded and disturbed patients. Two learning theories have received some support: one based upon positive reinforcers and one based on negative reinforcers.

Ferster (1961) noted that self-injurious behavior, such as head banging or face scratching, often receives positive reinforcement. These behaviors may be followed by increased attention from peers or from supervising adults. Even if the actual social interaction is, for example, verbal or physical punishment, this attention may be positively reinforcing as compared to the social neglect experienced if the self-injurious behavior is not emitted. Carr reviewed studies that showed that self-injurious behavior was less frequent when the child was alone. An alternative theory proposes that self-injurious behavior may be engaged in for the sensory stimulation it produces. This too may be viewed as a positive reinforcer.

Negative reinforcement can occur in situations, for example, in which the child, alone in his crib in the dark, bangs his head, and his parent arrives to investigate and turns on the light. Head banging is then followed by a reduced fear of the dark and being alone.

Some self-injurious behavior, such as wrist cutting, is often accompanied by feelings of relief, a negative reinforcer. The teenage female wrist-cutter often reports an increase in tension and the development of a trance-like state. After the cutting of the wrist, which can be painless, there is a reduction in the tension and a feeling of relief (Graff and Mallin, 1967).

These two theories receive some support from the fact that treatment techniques based upon these theories often help reduce the frequency of self-injurious behavior in children, though such techniques are not always successful (Carr, 1977; deCatanzaro, 1981).

Operant conditioning paradigms such as those described above for self-injurious behavior may similarly explain attempts at and threats of suicide. Suicidal behavior has often been viewed as a manipulative behavior. Indeed, Farberow and Shneidman's (1961) classic book on attempted suicide was called *The Cry For Help*, drawing attention to the desire to manipulate the environment by means of the suicidal act.

Sifneos (1966) studied attempted suicides and was struck by the manipulative aspects of their behavior: 66 percent were judged to have used manipulation (that is, tried to prevent another from leaving and thereby interrupting the relationship, or tried to control another person's actions in some way). Sifneos noted that the majority of these patients, were not motivated to receive psychotherapy and were usually satisfied with the results of their manipulative behavior, particularly if it had been effective. Sifneos noted that anxiety was often lacking in these patients and they appeared to be apathetic and fatalistic. Sifneos hypothesized that manipulative suicides were characterized by being more introspective, having few but intense relationships, having difficulty in expressing emotions, having exaggerated expections for themselves, being self-centered, and internalizing emotional problems.

Operant conditioning may similarly explain attempts at and threats of suicidal behavior. There are many possible positive reinforcers for suicidal behavior, including increased attention from significant others, expressions of concern (and even love), and the possibility of making others suffer. Negative reinforcers can include being removed from a stressful situation into a hospital (medical or psychiatric), and relief of tension. The reinforcement in the situations is obtained quite quickly, making it more potent.

The following is a case in which the suicide attempt was designed to elicit rejection from the environment:

> The attempted suicide was a male undergraduate who was disliked by most of those who met him. He displayed a "psychological sadism" toward others, finding pleasure in causing others to suffer. He attempted suicide during vacation time, when his roommate (who presumably liked him) was home and when he was living with others who knew him less well and did not like him. He took an overdose and then went down to the communal area of the dormitory to announce the fact. The others there barely listened and then went back to watching television. He went to bed and woke up 48 hours later. His roommate arrived back at the college and took him to the campus infirmary. When discussing this attempt, he said, "Those bastards let me die," yet he seemed pleased by the whole episode. When I looked at his psychological test results, his scores on the Buss and Durkee (1957) hostility inventory were high, especially on the Resentment Scale which measures a cynical and distrustful view of the world. His suicide attempt seemed designed to extort rejection from the others, carefully timed so that those who might rescue him were away. The rejection, once obtained, pleased him since it confirmed his view of the world.

Just as Lester (1972a) has suggested that suicide prevention centers may encourage suicide by publicizing the behavior, suicide prevention centers may positively reinforce suicidal behaviors by responding in a reinforcing manner when individuals contact them and describe suicidal symptoms.

The use of a suicide as a manipulative act, in order to extort particular responses from others, may lead to a sequence in which the severity of successive suicide actions has to increase in order to keep extorting the desired response from others. Lester, et al. (1978) found that attempted suicides who later completed suicide did indeed increase their suicidal intent (as measured by an objective scale based upon the circumstances of the suicidal act) in their final suicidal action from that on the earlier attempt. More detailed studies of the suicidal intent of repeated suicide attempters need to be carried out.

Such manipulative behavior may have been learned in childhood adolescence. A child may learn to hurt himself in order that he can manipulate others by getting a positive response from his parents to his self-injuries. For example, a parent who "suffers" because of misdeeds of his child, such as the child failing academic work, teaches the child that he can make others suffer (anxiety, grief, or rage) by doing things that admittedly are also self-injurious.

Suicide and Machiavellianism

One type of manipulativeness may be loosely described Machiavellianism, and Christie (1967) has devised a scale to measure this trait. High scorers on this scale are psychiatrists (as compared to other doctors) and those who win at poker-type games (as compared to those who lose). Lester (1968a) found that students who reported never having considered suicide did not differ from those who had attempted or threatened suicide in their scores on this scale. However, Lester (1970) found that on the Devries measure of suicide potential (Devries, 1966), high scorers did have higher Machiavellian scores than low scorers. Thus there may be an association between manipulativeness and suicidal potential. It is of interest to note that the manipulativeness of the suicidal person has been one of the most often discussed character traits in writings about suicide and yet no study has ever studied this variable intensively.

Discussion

Learning theories for self-injurious behavior have been proposed in the past. In this section, these paradigms have been extended to suicidal behavior and found to be useful. Suicidal behavior can be learned by operant conditioning. The notion of suicidal behavior as a manipulative act incorporates implicitly such a position. Manipulative behaviors are engaged in because they are reinforced by others.

Suicide as a Failure in Socialization

In most cultures suicide is frowned upon. Indeed, in some it is a sin. Furthermore, in any culture, suicide is rare. For example, Hungary has one of the highest suicide rates in the world. Yet its rate is only about 40 per 100,000 people per year. Suicide is always a statistically deviant act.

This suggests that suicidal individuals may be nonsocialized. Those who kill themselves have not been socialized into the traditional non-suicidal culture. Thus, on psychological tests of socialization and conformity, suicidal individuals should appear to be relatively unsocialized. Of course, Durkheim's (1951) ideas on suicide included the notion that suicide would be especially common in those who were relatively poorly socially integrated and poorly socially regulated. He called these types of suicide egoistic and anomic, respectively.

The absence of adequate parenting is also an important factor here. The quality of parenting can be poor, as in disorganized families. Or one or both parents can be absent, physically or psychologically. Jacobs (1971) has documented in detail the extremely disorganized family life of suicidal teenagers.

Religion is also a strong factor. Membership in a religious group will act against suicidal tendencies by providing a disapproving set of values for suicide and by providing social integration for the individual. Religious participation can also substitute for, in part, inadequate parenting. Finally, religious membership is a sign that the person has been adequately socialized.

This factor (of being poorly socialized into the traditional nonsuicidal culture) is necessary, but not a sufficient one. For the nonsocialized person, peers and role models provide a crucial input. Those who are nonsocialized will often be associated with other similarly nonsocialized people. Thus, this nonsocialized group forms its own small subculture. This subculture may share the information necessary for suicide. What methods to use? How many pills to take?

Role models, whether familiar friends or mythic heroes, provide models for nonconformity. When a Marilyn Monroe or Freddie Prinze completes suicide, they act as a role model for the ordinary person. And when one teenager in a school completes suicide, it occasionally leads to further suicides among the peer group.

The Chronic Suicide Attempter as a Social Deviant

Lester (1983) reviewed research on the person who makes repeated attempts at suicide. He concluded that the research shows them to be more often diagnosed as psychopathic or with a personality disorder, to be more often unemployed, to more often have a criminal record and to be more likely to be alcohol abusers. They seem to have a chronic maladaptive life-style and to be generally socially deviant.

Regional studies of attempted suicide also have found that rates are higher where indices of social disorganization are higher including overcrowding and poverty (Lester, 1983). Thus, it seems that the chronic attempter is a social deviant who comes from locales where social deviance is common. Families in these areas often fail to discipline their children and teach them the values of the larger society. They also fail to encourage them in interests and activities which would serve as deterrents to deviant behavior.

Such a child typically grows up without acquiring the attitudes and skills for achieving long-term goals. The person then turns to short-term methods for achieving goals, such as drugs, delinquent behavior, and suicide attempts. There may also be a sex difference here, with males choosing behaviors such as drugs and crime more often while females choose suicide attempts. (Females in these locales also have a high rate of illegitimate births.) A suicide attempt for such a person is a cathartic act and one which often brings about an immediate response from others.

An interesting question is why people in these locales turn to suicide rather than drugs or criminal behavior, given the predisposing factors. It may be that the choice is sex-linked as mentioned above. It may also be related to such factors as the availability of drugs in the area, the presence of a support group (or gang), and parental models.

Discussion

Suicide, no matter how much stress a person is under, is always a rare and, thus, a deviant act. It may, therefore, be heuristic to view the suicidal person as a nonsocialized individual, one who has failed to learn the normal cultural values, especially toward life and death.

A Learning Analysis of Suicide Considered as a Gambling Behavior

Suicide has often been considered to be a gamble. The suicidal individual often does not know whether or not he will die when he makes his suicide attempt. This can be because the factors affecting survival are not known fully. For example, the suicidal person may not be able to predict which potential rescuers will come by and intervene. Alternatively, the suicidal individual may not have sufficient information to know how to kill himself. What is a lethal dose of a particular medication, for example?

Lester and Lester (1971) noted that the seriously suicidal person does not know what death is like. He risks disappointment, but hopes for triumph or contentment. The mildly suicidal person may hope that his act will change his life, but he risks dying instead of awakening to an improved life. In addition to winning happiness or escaping from misery, the person may try suicide with the hope of preserving his threatened self-image. If he foresees severe illness, poverty, or mental disorder, he may use suicide to preserve the memory of himself as he was at his peak. This, again, is a gamble, especially since the disapproved act of suicide is likely to tarnish his image.

In Tikopia, Firth (1961) has described how people commit suicide by swimming out to sea. The suicidal individual can affect the chances of rescue and survival by choosing when to start swimming (late at night or early morning), how fast to swim, whether to swim directly out to sea or at an angle, and so on. Furthermore, the suicidal individual faces unpredictable factors such as when his absence will be discovered and whether the rescuers will make directly for where he is swimming. Thus, the suicidal attempt is a gamble, and the suicidal individual can affect the odds of survival by his choices.

Gambling behavior would appear at first sight to be inexplicable in terms of learning theory. Since gamblers in traditional gambling settings must lose in the end, it would appear that gambling behavior must eventually extinguish. However, as Frank (1979) has pointed out, a learning theory analysis can be proposed which goes far in explaining gambling behavior.

Reinforcing Suicidal Behavior

Frank (1979) noted that the effectiveness of rewards in shaping behavior depends upon several factors.

(1) The reinforcement should be delivered contingently. Reward should follow the target response and not occur when the response fails to appear.

When a person attempts suicide to achieve some response from the environment, often this is the only time when he does receive the response. A person who attempts suicide to prevent his lover from leaving or to get an expression of love from the lover typically does not get this response by conventional methods. Nothing seems to prevent the lover from leaving except attempting suicide.

(2) Early in the shaping of the behavior a very high proportion of the responses should be reinforced. After the behavior is established, a decrease in the proportion of responses reinforced will result in an increase in the overall response rate.

For suicide, this means that the first few suicide attempts must elicit the desired response. This is likely to occur because the significant other is usually made quite anxious by the first few attempts. However, eventually, the significant other gets immune to the suicidal talk, threats and attempts and does not respond every time. Thus, the reinforcement schedule switches from continuous to partial reinforcement as required for strong learning.

(3) Early in the development of the behavior large amounts of reinforcement should be applied. Later, gradual reductions in the amount of reward increase the response rate. (Sudden reductions in the amount of reinforcement, however, may decrease the response rate.)

This is very likely for suicidal behavior. The initial suicide threats and attempts will elicit the most reward, and the amount of reward should decrease with each successive suicidal threat or attempt. This is why the suicidal individual tends to increase the seriousness of successive suicidal threats and attempts.

(4) Responding in the absence of reinforcement will persist if the behavior was not rewarded each time it occurred in the past. Partial reinforcement leads to stronger resistance to extinction.

Again, the significant other typically responds the first time the person threatens or attempts suicide. He may not respond at once the next time. So the person makes continual threats, changing the content until the significant other responds a second time. And so on. Situations involving chronic continual suicidal threateners lead to the situation in which the significant other responds only some of the time, depending on the content of the threat, their own psychological state, and the social situation.

(5) Reinforcement should follow the response immediately.

Initially in the series of suicidal behaviors this is very likely to occur. For example, cases are common in which the suicidal person takes a handful of pills in front of the significant other who immediately intervenes, thereby reinforcing the behavior. Steer, et al. (1987) have studied suicide attempters who were actually interrupted in the course of their suicidal action (rather than afterwards) and found that these individuals have the highest likelihood of subsequent death from suicide.

(6) Resistance to extinction increases when it is hard to distinguish between the situations that produce reinforcement and those that do not.

Because of the complexities of human behavior, it is hard for the suicidal person to predict when the significant other will respond to the suicidal threat or attempt and when they will not. Furthermore, if we consider the type of person who will choose suicidal behavior as a means of manipulating the significant other, then he probably does not have good interpersonal skills. Thus, he may well find it harder to pre-dict the responses of significant others than those with superior inter-personal skills (who therefore have alternative strategies in their interpersonal interactions).

(7) Increased motivation results from increased responding.

Thus, as the other person emits more and more suicidal actions, then his motivation for behaving suicidally will increase.

It can be seen, therefore, that the basic laws of learning would predict that, for some people in some situations, the shaping of suicidal behav-ior by significant others would lead to strong learning and high rates of response (that is, emitting the suicidal behavior).

This analysis makes it possible to predict which individuals may engage in suicidal behavior for a while and then stop and which persist. The difference may lie in the way in which the significant others respond to the initial suicidal behaviors. Responding with a variable ratio rein-forcement schedule that changes over time in the appropriate manner (see point [2] above) will lead to the establishment of a chronic suicidal career.

The Effect of Punishment on Suicidal Behavior

Although punishment should eliminate behavior, there are situations under which the effects of punishment are minimized (Frank, 1979). In suicidal behavior, the punishment may include negative responses from significant others (although these may also involve attention, which may be rewarding) and the pain of the suicide attempt.

When is punishment ineffective?

(1) The punishment should be weak.

With regard to the pain of committing suicide, often the pain is not as intense as expected. A good analogy is touching your eyeball with your finger. For those who have never done this, it seems as if it will hurt. There is some anxiety about doing it. But you do it and find that it is almost painless. Thus, it becomes easier to do in the future.

The thought of slashing your wrists often elicits anticipatory pain. Yet remember how often you sliced your skin with a razor blade and never knew you had until you saw the blood on your skin. Slicing often does not hurt until sweat and dirt from the skin get into the cut.

Similarly, the negative responses from significant others are often mitigated in the earlier suicidal attempts by their concern for you and their anxiety. Furthermore, the punishment is accompanied by attention and concern which is rewarding.

Eventually, the punishing aspects of the significant other's response may outweigh the rewarding aspects, but initially this is less likely to be the case.

(2) For punishment to be ineffective, it should not be introduced at maximum strength, but start quite weakly.

For the response of the significant other to a suicidal threat or attempt, the initial response is unlikely to be at the fullest intensity. Thus, the punishment is likely to be ineffective.

(3) The frequency of the punishment should be low.

As seen from our analysis of the rewarding of suicide above, the punishment is unlikely to be given at a high frequency since rewarding the suicidal action by concern, attention and love competes with this response.

(4) An alternative response should not be available which elicits a reward greater than the punished response.

Suicidal people are typically in dysfunctional family systems in which alternative responses are not available which produce a reward greater than the punished response. Thus, suicidal behaviors are not eliminated.

(5) The delivery of punishment should become a signal for the availability of reinforcement.

For suicide, this means that the punishing responses from the significant others should be a signal that a reward is coming. Since the significant other often feels responsible and perhaps guilty for the suicidal individual's distress, the punishment may be accompanied by subtle signs of concern which signal the imminent delivery of positive responses from the significant other.

Thus, it can be seen that the punishment typically given to the suicidal person by his significant others does not meet the criteria for effective punishment. Therefore, it is not surprising that suicidal behavior is difficult to eliminate by means of punishment.

The Effect of Expectancies

Frank (1979) also points out the role that expectancies play in the learning of gambling behavior. Those who believe in the external control over the outcomes in their life are more likely to gamble.

We have seen elsewhere in this book the role that a belief in an external versus an internal locus of control for reinforcement might play in the determination of suicidal behavior. Those who believe in luck and fate as a major force in life may well commit suicide in a way that maximizes gambling aspects. I remember hearing of a case of a woman whose husband was having an affair with another woman, who took an overdose when her husband was out. She left a note downstairs telling him that she was upstairs after having taken an overdose. If he loved her, he would save her (by taking her to a hospital to get her stomach pumped) and she would live (and want to live). If he didn't love her, he could leave and let her die (or perhaps would stay out late again), and under those circumstances she would want to die. Thus, at the moment of her suicide attempt, she did not know whether she would live or die. The outcome was unpredictable.

Research has suggested that harsh discipline in childhood facilitates the development of a belief in an external locus of control (Phares, 1976). The child learns that others are extremely powerful and entirely control his rewards and punishments. This type of childhood experience may increase the likelihood of the appearance of suicide as a gambling behavior in adulthood.

Discussion

We can see that if suicidal behavior in some situations fits the model of a gambling behavior, then social learning theory can provide an understanding of how suicide as a gamble can occur.

Childhood Experiences of Punishment

There is some evidence that a child's experience of punishment may be critical in determining whether he learns to express his aggression outwards or whether he learns to inhibit this outward expression of aggression, turning it inward upon himself. In this section, theory and research on this topic will be reviewed and discussed.

Henry and Short's Theory

Henry and Short (1954) assumed that the basic and primary target of aggression is another person rather than the self. They then attempted to identify the sociological and psychological bases of the legitimization of other-oriented aggression. What enables the child to develop so that his primary response to frustration — that of other-oriented aggression — is seen as legitimate, while other children develop in such a way that this primary response is inhibited and self-directed aggression becomes legitimate?

Sociologically, the strength of external restraint was seen as the primary basis for the legitimization of other-oriented aggression. When behavior is required to conform rigidly to the demands and expectations of others, the share of others in the responsibility for the consequences of the behavior increases, thereby legitimizing other-oriented aggression. When external restraints are weak, the self must bear the responsibility for the frustration generated, and other-oriented aggression fails to be legitimized.

Henry and Short found two psychological correlates of other-oriented aggression in people — low superego strength and low guilt, and a specific type of cardiovascular reaction during stress similar to the effects of norepinephrine. They presented evidence to indicate that in the male child, these two factors are associated with the use of physical punishment as opposed to love-oriented punishment and punishment by the father rather than punishment by the mother. (Henry and Short never addressed their analysis to female children.)

Henry and Short then sought to show how experience of love-oriented punishment dealt out by the parent who is the source of nurturance and love leads to the development of tendencies to inhibit the primary, other-oriented expression of aggression. The argument centers around the idea that when the source of nurturance and love also administers the punishment, then the primary other-oriented expression of aggression threatens to end the flow of love and nurturance. If the child retaliates, he will receive no nurturance. Therefore, the child develops habits of inhibiting this primary other-oriented aggression.

Similarly, punishing a child by threatening to withdraw love also causes the child to inhibit his anger at being punished, since expression of that anger may lead also to loss of love.

Henry and Short explored the implications of their ideas for two topics: the suicide rates of the widowed and divorced and the suicide rates of murderers. They argued that the act of divorce is an expression of aggression against the spouse and that prior to the divorce the spouse was a primary source of nurturance and love. Therefore, for the divorced the consequence of aggression was loss of nurturance. For the widowed, the loss of love was a consequence of death and independent of aggression against the spouse. (Henry and Short did not admit that the widowed might have harbored hostile wishes against the deceased partner.) Henry and Short predicted, therefore, that the suicide rate should be higher in the divorced than in the widowed.

Henry and Short go on to predict that murderers who murder primary sources of love and nurturance will have higher suicide rates than murderers who do not murder such sources.

Research on Childhood Punishment and Suicide

Gold (1958) concentrated upon one aspect of Henry and Short's theory and examined the predictions that could be made from the assumption of a relationship between socialization experiences and the expression of aggression. Henry and Short had argued that experience of physical punishment led people to develop habits of expressing aggression outwardly whereas experience of love-oriented punishment led people to develop habits of expressing aggression inwardly. Gold argued that females were more likely to have experienced love-oriented punishment than were males, officers more than enlisted men, whites more than blacks, and urban dwellers more than rural dwellers. Thus females, officers, whites, and urban dwellers should all prefer inward-directed expression of aggression (including suicide) over outward-directed expression of aggression (including homicide) as compared to males, enlisted men, blacks, and rural dwellers respectively.

Gold felt that Henry and Short had been mistaken to use absolute rates of homicide and suicide, since the use of absolute rates did not allow a control to be applied for the total number of aggressive acts committed by a societal group. Gold suggested that a better measure was the suicide rate divided by the combined suicide and homicide rate. When Gold tested his predictions using this measure of the preference for suicide as compared to homicide in the groups under investigation, his predictions were confirmed for all four pairs of groups.

Gold's suggestion makes good sense. However, Lester (1967) tested the relationship between socialization experiences and the incidence of suicide and homicide in a sample of primitive societies and failed to find the predicted association regardless of whether he used absolute rates or relative rates of suicide and homicide. The failure of Lester to confirm Gold's results may reflect upon the validity of the postulated relationship between socialization experiences and suicidal behavior, upon the measures suggested by Gold, or upon the methodological inadequacies of Lester's study. (Lester was unable to use a random sample of societies but instead had to use societies for which the required data could be located.)

Lester (1968b) compared the recollection of their childhood punishment experiences of attempted and threatened suicides and nonsuicidal college students and found no differences. However, the recollection of early punishment experiences is, in all probability, invalid as a measure of actual childhood experiences.

More General Learning Experiences

The learning experiences of childhood may be more general than those mentioned above. For example, Hendin (1965) attributed the difference in the suicide rates between Sweden and Norway to differences in personality. But he attributed the differences in personality, in turn, to differences in child rearing in the two countries. The children in the two countries acquire different goals and different strategies for coping.

Theorists such as Eysenck (1970) see the superego, as defined by psychoanalysts, as a simple result of classical conditioning. Acts associated with punishment become classically conditioned to fear and pain, the results of the punishment. The child then learns to avoid these acts. If a parent is overly harsh in raising the child, the child may develop an overly strong superego subset of wishes (Toman, 1960). This may lead to high levels of depression and guilt in adulthood, whose source is often unconscious since the individual may have repressed the id desires seeking expression *and* the superego desires forbidding their expression. Such an individual may well feel a need for punishment to assuage the feelings of guilt, especially if the source of the guilt is unconscious and cannot be assuaged by conscious rational means.

Menninger (1938) described three types of motives for suicide: to die, to kill, and to be killed. In the desire to be killed, the individual, typically depressed, feels guilty and worthless and completes suicide as a pennance and atonement for his sins. This motive for suicide may be especially strong in those who have been through the process described above.

Suicide as a Result of the Ineffectiveness of Adaptive Coping Skills

Jacobs (1971) has presented a thorough study of the progressive disintegration of the life of the suicidal adolescent. He looked at the number and type of debilitating events experienced by suicidal and nonsuicidal adolescents and found that although the suicidal adolescents had experienced a greater total number of such events (for example, residence moves, break up of romances, hospitalizations, and so on), the difference in the frequency of such events was most marked after the onset of adolescence. Thus not only were the suicidal adolescents subjected to a more extensive and intensive history of problems, but also the problems did not diminish in adolescence.

To investigate how the adolescents attempted to cope with the events that they experienced, Jacobs looked at the onset of behavioral problems

during adolescence. The suicidal adolescents had experienced significantly more behavioral problems than the control adolescents. Both
groups resorted to behavior problems classified as "rebellion" to the
same degree. The suicidal adolescents, however, tended to show "withdrawal into self" and "physical withdrawal" significantly more than the
control adolescents. Jacobs interpreted this withdrawal to indicate the
alienation of the suicidal adolescent from his parents. Jacobs also found
that the suicidal adolescents had a greater onset of behavioral problems
during adolescence (that is, during the escalation phase).

Jacobs found that the difference in the perception of behavior problems by the adolescent and by the parent was similar for both groups of
adolescents. However, possibly because the suicidal adolescent showed
more behavioral problems, he felt more inappropriately disciplined than
did the nonsuicidal adolescent. Jacobs noted that while the parent
viewed behavioral problems as simply problems, the adolescents also
saw them as adaptive techniques in dealing with the problems in his
family. Thus he was often disappointed when his parents failed to perceive the behavior problem in this way, and this increased his alienation.
The suicidal adolescent was subjected to more kinds of disciplinary techniques that the nonsuicidal adolescent and, in particular, more nagging,
yelling, witholding approval, and whipping. The suicidal adolescent appeared to feel as a result of this that he was subject to unfair discipline
and rejection. The parent felt frustrated in not being able to contain the
behavior problems, and the final result was to increase the alienation between parent and adolescent.

Jacobs found that the adolescents generally used adaptive techniques
in trying to deal with the problems at home before turning maladaptive
techniques such as running away and attempting suicide. Only one
adolescent attempted suicide without ever resorting to other techniques
(and his problems were different in that they stemmed from ill-health
primarily).

Thus, these suicidal adolescents turned to suicide because their significant others failed to respond to the more adaptive coping skills.

Suicide as a Result of Failure to Learn Appropriate Coping Skills

Leonard (1967) proposed a developmental theory of suicide that
stressed the importance of the second and third years of life during
which the child begins a struggle for independence and autonomy from
his mother. If the child's growth as an individual is blocked, he may not

develop adequate impulse control, coming to rely more on external controls. Leonard felt that poor impulse control was likely to lead in adulthood to acting-out, including the acting-out of suicidal impulses. Leonard also felt that problems during this stage of development led to a rigid adherence to one pattern of responding and a lack of flexibility in responding to situations. Later in life, when the suicidal individual finds himself in a crisis, not only is he unable to find a solution, but also he is unable to accept compromises, changes and defeats. This tendency has been noted by Neuringer (1964) in his research.

Discussion

In this section, we have looked at the evidence that childhood punishment and more general rearing experiences may play a role in determining whether the child develops a depressive or an assaultive life style. In particular, punishment by the same parent, who is the source of nurturance and punishment using love-oriented techniques, were proposed as experiences likely to lead to depressed and suicidal life styles.

Societal Shaping of Suicidal Behavior

Societal Condemnation of Suicide

The notion is often advanced that completed suicide is more common where societal condemnation of suicide is low. This was proposed by Dublin and Bunzel (1933) and more recently by Farber (1968). Farber hypothesized that this factor might account for the low suicide rate among Catholics and that it might play a part in determining the difference in the suicide rate of the Danes and the Norwegians, a problem with which he was concerned. The Danes condemned suicide less and had the higher suicide rate.

The societal condemnation of suicide has also been used to account for the low suicide rate in Moslem nations. However, evidence indicates that a great deal of under-reporting of suicide occurs in Moslem nations (Headley, 1983).

Douglas (1967) examined the difference in the suicide rates of Catholics and Protestants in some detail.

Douglas noted that there were subcultural differences in the attempts to conceal suicidal deaths. Since suicide is condemned more severely by Catholics than by Protestants, one would expect the reported suicide rate among Catholics to be lower than the reported rate among Protestants and this is indeed found. There is no direct evidence on the relative tendencies of religious groups to attempt to conceal suicidal deaths. However, a study by Waldstein (1934) is of interest here. In his study of the different cantons of Switzerland, he noted that the Catholic cantons had a higher proportion of accidental deaths than did the Protestant cantons while the Protestant cantons had a higher proportion of suicidal deaths. Similarly, Ferracuti (1957) noted that as one moves from the South to the North in Italy, there is a steady decrease in the importance of the Catholic organization and a steady increase in the official suicide rate. Douglas also noted that the degree of urbanization increases as one moves north, as does the degree of industry in the areas and the wealth and education of the citizens, so that the data could be interpreted to mean that urban-industrial, wealthy-educated areas have more efficient officials gathering statistics.

Despite the cogency of Douglas's arguments, it remains true that suicide rates for immigrants to the USA and to Australia from countries such as Ireland and Spain remain low here in comparison to other immigrant groups, though suicides from all immigrant groups are examined by American (or Australian) medical examiners (Lester, 1972c; Sainsbury and Barraclough, 1968). For example, in 1959, Irish immigrants to the USA had the eleventh rate out of twelve immigrant groups (Dublin, 1963). (Only Mexico was lower.)

In an attempt to test the notion that societal approval of suicide facilitates the occurrence of suicide, Lester (1983a) used data from nine regions of the USA whose inhabitants were surveyed and asked about their approval of suicide. There was no association between the approval of suicide in each region and the region's suicide rate. However, such a study of a small number of respondents in a few regions does not constitute an adequate study of the issue, but merely serves as a stimulus for subsequent research.

Since suicide is an action in conflict with most major religious teachings, suicide is contrary to the dominant moral philosophy of societies. Thus, suicides are deviating from societal norms and so are deviants.

Societal Expectations

Societal expectations have been introduced as an explanation for suicidal behavior in only one area, that of sex differences in suicidal behavior.

One clear phenomenon in suicidal behavior is that males complete suicide more than females, whereas females attempt suicide more than males. This phenomenon occurs in almost all nations of the world and in almost all subgroups of the population in any nation (Lester, 1979).

Several explanations have been proposed for this phenomenon. The major one is that males chose different methods for suicide from females and that the methods males choose are more lethal (that is, more likely to result in death) than those chosen by females. For example, males use firearms more, while females use medications more.

Linehan (1973) asked what happens once a person has reached the crisis point where suicide is seen as a viable alternative. Then the social acceptability of suicidal behavior becomes a factor. If attempted suicide is seen as a "weak" or as a "feminine" behavior, then men may be less likely to choose that alternative. Men, therefore, may not have a means of communicating mild levels of distress and so be more likely to suppress their depression and self-destructive impulses until they are so strong as to precipitate a lethal self-destructive behavior.

Linehan tested her ideas by presenting to undergraduate students case studies involving males and females in crisis and varying the characteristics of the patients so that some were portrayed as "masculine" while others were portrayed as "feminine." She found that the students predicted suicide as an outcome more often for males than for females, and also that suicide was the predicted outcome more often for masculine patients than for feminine patients. The students predicted suicide 71 percent of the time for the masculine males, 62 percent of the time for masculine females, 43 percent of the time for feminine males, and 22 percent of the time for feminine females.

This suggests that sex role expectations, may function as to shape sex differences in suicidal behavior.

Discussion

No good study of the societal shaping of suicide has appeared, but there are suggestions for future research. It has been suggested that societal condemnation of suicide does inhibit suicidal behavior, but no sound study of this possibility has been conducted. Only one study has been conducted on societal stereotypes and expectations about sex differences in suicidal behavior, and it found that these expectations paralleled the actual differences between male and female suicidal behavior.

The Role of the Family in Shaping Suicidal Behavior

Apart from those who are truly alone, a suicidal individual exists in a network of family and friends. The people in this social network often play a critical role in shaping the person's suicidal behavior. Even those who live alone and are relatively socially isolated grew up with family and friends, and the foundation of their suicidal behavior may still have been shaped by these early experiences.

Freud's theory of suicide made loss the central experience. In depression, the one who has been loved is lost and incorporated into the person's mind by identification, in a process called ego-splitting. If this lost person was also hated, then the anger is turned inward upon the incorporated representation of the lost one and, therefore, upon the self. Freud also felt that it was the anxiety that was aroused by the separation (or threatened separation) that was the critical factor.

Richman (1986) has noted that separation experiences occur in the whole family, and the anxiety may be felt by all. Furthermore, these separation experiences and their anxiety may be handed down from generation to generation.

Richman pointed out that suicidal people may be those who experienced early loss which then sensitized them to later loss, and Lester and Beck (1976) found empirical support for this notion.

In families, not everyone is permitted to separate. Richman noted that it is the one who is the target for this separation anxiety who may become suicidal. The responsibility for the survival of the family is placed on this one individual, who therefore must not be allowed to leave, while other family members are permitted more autonomy.

Often suicidal family members have symbiotic relationships with one another, in which they depend upon one another for exploitation and for the satisfaction of neurotic needs.

The Shaping of Deviant Behavior

It is easy to document how parents shape deviant behavior in their children. Richman gave an example of a mother who, when told that her high-school daughter had been caught in a homosexual act, was shocked but took the daughter out to a fancy restaurant and to buy her clothes, clearly rewarding the daughter for her homosexuality. (A homosexual daughter would not leave her mother to get married!)

Federn noted that no one kills himself whose death has not been desired by another (Maddison and Mackey, 1966). Meerloo (1962) made a similar point, that those who kill themselves are wished dead by others. Meerloo described cases in which the suicide was clearly encouraged in his suicide by another, albeit unconsciously, a situation that he called *psychic homicide* (murdering another by getting them to commit suicide).

Richman noted many instances in which parents made clearly murderous statements to their children who had attempted suicide, in the presence of the psychologist! For example, a father of a 16 year-old girl said to her "Why don't you kill yourself. At least we'd know where you are." Richman notes that this statement illustrates that this particular father feared the loss of his daughter, indicating a symbiotic relationship.

The hostility may be less obvious, but nonetheless present. Richman describes the case of a 78 year-old man who told his wife he was going to kill himself and tried to kiss her goodbye. Her reaction was to turn away and leave the house to go shopping. When she got home, he had cut his throat. In another case, a daughter took an overdose of pills, went and laid beside her father in bed and told him. The father went back to sleep and when he awoke the next morning left his daughter lying there to go to work.

Even more extreme cases are presented by Richman, closely resembling murder. In one, a mother was upset over her 14 year-old daughter's drug use and undesirable friends. One night her 15 year-old brother made his sister take an overdose of pills after she had upset their mother. In another, a woman had a mystic revelation that her son, a drug addict with whom she lived, had to die. She went to his room and made him take a bottle of pills. (Richman notes that the mother was not psychotic.)

Scapegoating

Family therapists have long been aware that pathological families often select one family member as the scapegoat, the one who will bear the symptoms of the pathology. Richman noted that the scapegoating can be total, in which the scapegoat is blamed for all of the problems in the family. The function of this scapegoating is, of course, to help the family avoid dealing with unbearable problems. In suicidal situations, the scapegoating is used to prevent separation. In one case, an 18 year-old son could not leave home as he claimed to desire because he was taking drugs and was suicidal. Even the son agreed with this conclusion, indicating his own difficulty in separating. In another case, a son heard his parents say that they would divorce once he left for college. Soon after arriving at college, he attempted suicide and had to return home.

Discussion

It can be seen that families shape the behavior of their suicidal members. The person's suicidal behavior serves to satisfy his own desires and those of his family members. All benefit from his suicidal preoccupations or actions, and often all act so as to reward his suicidal behavior and punish alternative behaviors. Thus, the suicidal individual learns well from his family and often conforms to their explicit and implicit demands.

Subcultural Factors in Teenage Suicide

The concept of "subcultures" has been very popular in theories of criminal and delinquent behavior. A subculture is a culture that exists within a larger culture. A subculture has its own customs, values and attitudes. The subculture shapes behaviors, rewarding some while punishing others. Consequently, subcultures are critically dependent upon the social pressures exerted by others, both directly and indirectly (via introjected values and desires).

The concept of subcultures has been used extensively to explain delinquency (Cohen, 1955), violence (Wolfgang and Ferracuti, 1969), and drug abuse (Johnson, 1973).

Most previous theories of subcultures have focused on whole regions of the USA, such as the theory that there is a Southern subculture (Gastil, 1971), or on a whole socioeconomic class. Subculture theories of delinquency often focus on small groups, such as the gang (Cohen, 1955). To apply subcultural theory to suicidal behavior in teenagers further reduces the size of the group involved. A group of depressed and suicidal teenagers is often quite small, in the case to be presented in this section, only five teenagers. However, these five teenagers shared values and attitudes that are common in other teenagers, so that the subculture can be seen as quite large if we focus on all of those that share the attitudes and values.

Lester (1987) presented a case from a small town in Pennsylvania, in which three teenagers from a group of five completed suicide. He noted several elements of a teenage suicidal subculture. There was heavy drug involvement, relations with parents that were either full of intense resentment or apparent indifference. There was poor self-image, including components of unworthiness and feelings of ugliness, with symptoms of shyness and dependency on another (or a small number of peers). There was also loss of a lover (though there was no report on the sexual relations between members of the group). There was a great involvement with the fantasies engendered by heavy metal music and day dreams of being a musician of similar ilk and fame.

Although this group was quite self-contained, their suicides generated a great deal of suicidal preoccupation and acting-out in their peers. This suggests that the subcultural values were quite widespread. Interestingly, hostility was also aroused. One girl overdosed on Tylenol and, on her return to school, found a full bottle of Tylenol in her locker with a note saying, "Do it right next time." After Marc's suicide, someone wrote on Michelle's locker, "You killed him."

These five teenagers were clearly in a "peer group." However, the fact that their behaviors tapped into a suicidal vein among the other students in the high school points to the existence of a "peer culture" that transcends the peer group. Within each peer group, competition for status frequently occurs, and this leads to experimentation with new behaviors. Thus, behaviors within a peer group (and thus the peer culture) tend to become more extreme. In a suicidal subculture, overt suicidal acts seem inevitable in time. The existence of large numbers of peer groups in the peer subculture and the experimenting by peer groups with new behaviors mean that the subculture is dynamic over time, continually being modified. Therefore, the teenage suicidal subculture in the next decade may be significantly different from the present subculture.

The subculture is an important concept since it sharpens our awareness of what the values and attitudes are that accompany participation in a particular type of behavior, and it draws our attention to the social shaping of behavior that can take place, facilitating the entry of people into the subculture and maintaining their presence in the subculture after entry.

Learning Influences in the Methods Chosen
for Suicide

The method chosen for suicide has not interested researchers much in the past, but it provides important evidence for the learning influences in suicidal behavior.

Hirsh (1960) reported on fads for methods of suicide. Gas was very popular in the early 1900s, and "to take the pipe" became a common phrase. Plastic bags were used more often following reports of accidental deaths by suffocation soon after their invention. Church and Phillips (1984) have reported on clusters of suicides in a town in Great Britain, using plastic bags that suggests imitation of method. In the 1960s and 1970s, suicide by self-immolation has become popular (Ashton and Donnan, 1979). Since two-thirds of them have had a political motivation (Crosby, et al., 1977), the influence of Buddhist monks in Vietnam immolating themselves to protest the political situation there seems to be influential.

The Methods Chosen by Immigrants

Burvill, et al. (1973) reported on the methods for suicide used by suicides in England and Wales and compared these with the methods used by immigrants from those countries when they arrive in Australia. They found that the immigrants switched from the British pattern to the Australian pattern. Burvill, et al. (1982, 1983) showed a similar trend in immigrants to Australia from some other countries. For example, 52 percent of Australian males completing suicide used active methods. In contrast, 32 percent of native English males and 79 percent of native Irish males used active methods. However, in immigrants to Australia, 43 percent of English males and 57 percent of Irish males used active methods, a move toward the Australian pattern.

Suicide Venues

There are many famous suicide venues around the world. Two popular ones in the USA are Niagara Falls (Lester and Brockopp, 1971) and the Golden Gate Bridge in San Francisco.

Seiden and Spence (1983-1984) have demonstrated convincingly the role of learning in this phenomenon. They noted that the Bay Bridge is only six miles away from the Golden Gate Bridge, was completed six months before the Golden Gate Bridge, and is the same height. From 1937-1979, 672 people have jumped off the Golden Gate Bridge as compared to only 121 off the Bay Bridge. The bridges do differ in that only the Golden Gate Bridge allows pedestrians. However, even when pedestrians are excluded, the number of suicides from the Golden Gate Bridge still exceeds the number of suicides from the Bay Bridge by 325 to 107.

Seiden and Spence noted that suicides from the Bay Bridge are rarely publicized whereas suicides from the Golden Gate Bridge are still occasionally noted on the front pages of newspapers. The Golden Gate Bridge is noted for its suicide by Gray Line tours and by the Golden Gate National Recreation Area Guidebook. Some people bet on the day when the next jump will occur.

Seiden and Spence noted that East Bay residents, who jumped off the bridges to their death and who drove to the bridges, have to drive over the Bay Bridge to get to the Golden Gate Bridge. However, 50 percent of East Bay jumpers do just this. Seiden and Spence concluded that the Golden Gate Bridge has become a symbol, possibly romantic, for suicides. There were no cases of suicides from Marin County crossing the Golden Gate Bridge in order to jump off the Bay Bridge. Furthermore, all of the jumpers from outside of California jumped off the Golden Gate Bridge.

Thus, it seems clear that the choice of people to jump off the Golden Gate Bridge is affected by learning.

Experience with Methods for Suicide

Marks and Stokes (1976) compared undergraduate students in Georgia and in Wisconsin. For both the males and females, more students in Georgia had owned a gun than students in Wisconsin. Furthermore, the Georgia students were much more likely than Wisconsin students to have had parents who owned guns and to have fired a gun as a child. Having a parent or relative who owned a gun was also positively associated with having fired a gun.

Thus, it seems clear that southern people have more experience with guns from childhood on. Marks and Abernathy (1974) used an index of southernness for the different regions of the USA and found that, the more southern a region was, the higher was the proportion of suicides using guns. Thus, experience with guns seems to lead to their increased use for suicide.

Again, this evidence supports the influence of learning to the determination of a choice of method for suicide. Furthermore, the sex difference in familiarity with and use of guns is even stronger than the regional difference.

Culturally Determined Types of Suicides

Durkheim (1951) proposed four types of suicide based on two underlying dimensions of social constraints. First, suicide was seen as more likely if the degree of social integration of the individual into the society was very high or very low. Second, suicide was seen as more likely if the social regulation of the individual by the society was very weak or very strong. Later writers, such as Johnson (1965), have noted that it is very difficult to distinguish between social integration and social regulation since the two processes tend typically to occur together. People who are strongly integrated socially tend also to be highly regulated socially.

Be that as it may, some forms of suicide do seem to be a result of extremely strong social pressures. For example, the practice of suttee in some Indian subcultures, in which the wife dies on the funeral pyre of her husband, would seem to be determined by strong social pressures. It should be noted that often this form of suicide is willingly undergone, since the women have learned the cultural traditions well. So too seppuku, the ritual disembowelment carried out by Japanese who have disgraced themselves, may be seen as a learned cultural tradition.

DeCatanzaro (1981) has also noted the culturally unique methods for suicide that can be found. For example, in Tikopia, suicide is accomplished by hanging in an unusual way. The person uses a fine cord to make a noose, which is then tied to one part of his house. He then rushes to another part of the house, whereupon the fine cord brings death quickly as it tightens around his neck. The suicide often refrains from food intake for a day before killing himself so that he will not defecate on dying.

Suicide and the Use of Tools

Suicide is linked to a capacity to use tools. DeCatanzaro (1981) suggested that this is why suicide is difficult to show in animals, for humans are one of the few species clearly able to use tools.

The methods for suicide typically are the result of human technological innovations. These methods and their effects have to be learned. Suicide by hanging, fire, cutting and piercing instruments, poisons derived from plants, and firearms all involve the use of tools. Only drowning, jumping and exposure to harsh environments do not involve the use of tools and technology.

DeCatanzaro (1981) has suggested that suicide may be rare in primitive societies because such societies are less technologically advanced. Morselli (1882) also suggested that completed suicide increases in frequency in more civilized societies. However, suicide is estimated very differently in primitive societies. In developed countries it is possible to carry out a count of the individuals in a population dying from suicide each year. In less developed societies we have to use rough methods such as judgments made by readers of ethnographers' reports of the frequency of suicide.

It appears, however, that there is a large variation in the suicide rates of primitive societies, and Hoskin et al. (1969) reported finding a very high rate of suicide (23 per 100,000 per year) in Kandrian in New Britain (an island in New Guinea). The most usual method of suicide in this society was hanging, and the method seemed to be ritualized. It was customary to place three knots in the rope that would impinge upon the trachea and the two carotid arteries. In other primitive societies ethnographers have reported the absence of suicidal behavior (for example, among the Zuni). Whether primitive societies and modern societies differ in general is not known at the present time due to the difficulty in comparing the different kinds of data from the two kinds of societies.

Discussion

The choice of method for suicide is clearly affected by cultural factors. Furthermore, these cultural factors are not simply a result of availability of a particular method, for the way an available method is used for suicide is also shaped by the culture. Thus, this evidence strongly supports a social learning theory for suicides.

Suicide in Significant Others

A social learning theory of suicide would be immeasurably strengthened if it could be shown that suicidal behavior was frequent in the families, relatives and friends of suicidal individuals. This would provide the basis for an imitation effect. It would give the suicidal person a chance to learn about suicide as a strategy by watching others engage in the behavior and by observing the effects of the behavior. What evidence is there for this?

Six reports have appeared which report an excess of suicides in the families, relatives and friends of suicidal people: Corder, et al., 1974; Diekstra, 1974; Garfinkel, et al., 1979; Hauschild, 1968; Murphy, et al., 1969; Woodruff, et al., 1972. On the other hand, eight studies have found no differences: Doroff, 1969; Finlay, 1970; Hill, 1969; Johnson and Hunt, 1979; Pokorny, 1960; Rorsman, 1973; Rosen, 1970; Tucker and Reinhardt, 1966.

In addition, Pollack (1938) compared attempted suicides with completed suicides and found a greater incidence of completed suicide in the families of the completed suicides. Ettlinger (1964) compared attempted suicides who subsequently killed themselves with those who did not and found no significant differences in the incidence of completed suicide in the family members.

Winokur et al. (1973) compared depressed inpatients with an early onset of the disorder to those who had a late onset of the disorder. The early onset patients had more parents who had completed suicide than the late onset patients had. This was especially so for the female patients.

It is sometimes difficult to make sense of research that is inconsistent. Six studies found an excess of suicidal behavior in the significant others of suicidal people, while eight studies found no differences. Perhaps it is noteworthy that no study found a lower incidence of suicide in the significant others of suicidal individuals? The fourteen studies, therefore, seem to indicate an excess (albeit a modest excess) of suicidal behavior in the significant others of suicidal people.

One final study seems especially pertinent to the present discussion.

Sletten et al. (1973) found an excess of attempted suicides (but not completed suicides) in the relatives of attempted suicides and an excess of completed suicides (but not attempted suicides) in the relatives of completed suicides. No one appears to have tried to replicate the specificity of this result, but, if it proves replicable, it would provide powerful evidence for a social learning theory of suicide.

Suicide in the Social Networks of the Suicidal Individual

Kreitman et al. (1969) predicted that those who had attempted suicide would have more kin and close friends who were suicidal than would nonsuicidal individuals. They traced a sample of contacts of attempted suicides and found a greater incidence of suicide attempts than would be expected on the basis of chance in these contacts. The phenomenon was especially strong in those less than 35 years of age and in those attempting suicide with drugs. These data could indicate either the effects of suggestion and imitation or merely the mutual attraction between suicidal individuals.

Discussion

There appears to be good evidence that suicidal behavior is common in the relatives and friends of suicidal people. However, it is far from clear why the results of the different studies are inconsistent. Furthermore, the importance of the type of suicidal behavior is not well established. That is, do attempted and completed suicides have different patterns of suicidal behavior in their significant others? Sletten's result that completed suicide had an excess of completed suicide in significant others while attempted suicides had an excess of attempted suicides is intriguing, but in need of replication.

The Role of Suggestion in Suicide

Lester (1972) noted several lines of evidence for the effects of suggestion on suicide: the influence of newspaper publicity, epidemics of suicidal behavior, fashions in the methods for suicides, and suicidal behavior in friends and relatives. In this section, we shall focus on newspaper publicity, epidemics of suicidal behavior, and suicide pacts.

Newspaper Strikes

It is often said that suicidal behavior can be elicited in people by telling them of other suicides or by having them imitate another's actions. It has frequently been alleged, for example, that newspaper reports of suicidal behavior can precipitate suicidal behavior in others. Motto (1967) attempted to test this particular assertion by examining the suicide rates in seven cities in the United States which had suffered from newspaper strikes that eliminated all newspapers (save those brought in from other cities). Motto found that the suicide rate was lower during the strike than in previous years in five cities and higher in two cities., but in each case the difference was not significant. Motto concluded that there was no evidence that newspaper reporting of suicidal behavior increases by suggestion the incidence of suicide in the readers of the newspaper.

Blumenthal and Berger (1973) also found no effect from a newspaper strike (affecting half of the city's newspapers) on the suicide rate in New York City in 1966. On the other hand, Motto (1970) found that the suicide rate dropped during a newspaper strike in Detroit but for women only. The drop was found for all age groups.

Newspaper Publicity

Barraclough, et al. (1977) found an increase in the number of suicides in Portsmouth, England, after a newspaper story about a suicide, but this increase was found only for males below the age of forty-four.

Phillips (1974) found that front page newspaper stories on suicide increased the number of suicides in the following month. The rise was found only in the region served by the newspaper. Phillips found no increase in the number of suicides in the month following a presidential death. There was no subsequent dip in the number of suicides each month, and so Phillips concluded that newspaper publicity creates additional suicides rather than speeding up suicide in those who would have killed themselves anyway.

Phillips (1977) also found an increase in motor vehicle accidents in the week after a front page newspaper story on suicide. Again, the rise was limited to the region served by the newspaper. Phillips (1978) found that combined murder/suicide incidents reported in the press were followed in the next week by an increase in multifatality airplane accidents (but not single fatality airplane accidents). (This effect was not found after television publicity of homicide/suicide incidents.) Phillips (1979) found an increase in single vehicle car accidents after a front page story on suicide. Murder/suicide stories were followed by an increase in multi-vehicle crashes. The correlation between the age of the suicide in the newspaper story and the age of the driver in the single car crashes was positive, suggesting that people of the same age as the suicide were more likely to be influenced. For a single vehicle crash after a suicide story, the time interval between the crash and the death was shorter, suggesting that the crash was more serious (and therefore perhaps suicidally motivated). Bollen and Phillips (1981) replicated this increase in motor vehicle fatalities after a publicized suicide.

There have been several critiques of Phillips's research, but no alternative analyses of his data have been presented. Thus, it seems very likely that newspaper publicity of suicide stories does cause a rise in the suicide rate in the following week.

Suicide on Television

Phillips (1982) studied the effects of suicides in soap operas on suicide in the general population. He found more suicides (and motor vehicle fatalities) in the week in which a soap opera suicide occurred as compared to the previous week. Bollen and Phillips (1982) next looked at the effect of television news coverage of actual suicides. Again, they found an increase in the number of suicides in the following week as compared to the previous week.

Epidemics of Suicide

Imitation does appear to play a role in "epidemics" of suicidal behavior. Hankoff (1961) reported an epidemic of attempted suicide in a Marine base overseas. The attempts were clustered in time, and the methods used were similar in each cluster. Examination of one cluster in detail showed that the first attempt had resulted in maximum secondary gain (hospitalization and removal from duty), whereas the last attempt resulted in the least secondary gain. Hankoff implied that, as rewards from attempting suicide declined, the Marines dropped that behavior as a means of procuring relief. Crawford and Willis (1966) found evidence of imitation in three pairs of suicides that took place in a hospital, but no evidence in three other pairs of suicides. Niemi (1975) found that completed suicides in Finnish prisons occurred within two days of each other more often than would be expected by chance. Coleman (1987) has reported many cases of suicide clusters that appear to show imitation, including many recent clusters of teenagers, but some investigators doubt that all clusters reflect imitation (Selkin, 1986).

Seiden (1968) investigated five completed suicides who jumped off buildings at the University of California in Berkeley during a one-month period. Seiden felt that the suicides were not imitation because (a) all the individuals appeared to have a history of severe mental disturbance, (b) the epidemic stopped as abruptly as it had begun, and (c) none of the five suicides knew one another. It is obvious that these arguments do not logically rule out the possibility of imitation, but this report does suggest that we look closely at suicides clustered together in time to see if they could be independent and occurring close together by chance.

In a study of people jumping off the Golden Gate Bridge, Kirch and Lester (1986a) found no temporal clustering of the jumps. However, in an analysis of data provided by Church and Phillips (1984) of suicides using plastic bags in Britain, a clear clustering effect was found (Kirch and Lester, 1986b).

Suicide Pacts

It is not clear in the case of a suicide pact whether a normally non-suicidal individual is made to commit suicide as a result of suggestion from the partner. It is more likely that two disturbed individuals become tied together in a pathological relationship. Incidentally, Cohen (1964) found that the majority of pacts were between husbands and wives (about 72 percent) and not between lovers.

Mass Suicides

Mass suicides are rare, but the spectacle of large numbers of people completing suicide together is profoundly upsetting. The recent mass suicide of several hundred people at Jonestown in Guyana in 1978, even though coercion (and even murder) may have played a role, illustrates the power of contagion.

Discussion

This evidence clearly indicates the role of suggestion. The studies by Phillips on newspaper publicity provide the first good support for the possibility that suicidal behavior is affected by suggestion. The appropriate controls were included in the research design, and the results are open to few other explanations.

DeCatanzaro (1981) has argued that these suggestion effects are shown in only a minority of suicides, since most suicides are relatively isolated acts. This isolation, of course, does not rule out suggestion, as we do not know how this particular individual making an isolated suicide attempt acquired the idea that suicide was an option for him. We do not know what he read in the media or which suicides he heard about (or at what age these influences took place). DeCatanzaro also noted that even suicides in clusters may be motivated by personal difficulties and stress. But people have different ways of responding to stress and intrapsychic problems. Suggestion and imitation may well affect the choice of response once the stress has occurred.

Conclusions

The evidence that suicide is, at least in part, a learned behavior is overwhelming. The learning model for psychopathology is a popular explanation for disturbed behavior (and this model is compatible with labelling theory). It was noted that the cognitive theories of psychotherapy lend strong support for a social learning theory of depression since these therapies focus on the cognitive mediators (thoughts) that can create severe depression. Since suicidal behavior is commonly associated with depression, the learning theories of depression have immediate applicability to suicide.

Self-injurious behavior also appears to be, in part, a learned behavior, affected by the response that the self-injurious behavior elicits from the environment. Similarly, non-lethal suicidal behavior typically elicits a response from the environment that can serve to reinforce the behavior. Interestingly here, it is attempted suicide which is more likely to be affected by reinforcement from the environment. However, if the reinforcement stops, then the suicide attempter may be tempted to increase the risk and lethality involved in the suicide attempts, eventually leading to completed suicide. It may be that extinction will not necessarily eliminate non-lethal suicidal behavior, but rather serve to increase its lethality.

Although there have been many suggestions that childhood experiences play a role in suicidal behavior, ideas which figure strongly in Henry and Short's theory of suicide, there is little research on this topic. It is time that more effort was put into research on the childhood experiences of suicidal individuals.

The presence of learning factors in suicide is supported by the influence of societal attitudes toward suicide. This variable has long figured in theories of suicide, and indeed nations with a dominant religious philosophy that strongly condemns suicide do have a low suicide rate. Although there is not yet good research support for the influence of societal attitudes toward suicide, societal attitudes play such a large role in determining human behavior in general that it is unlikely that they do not play a role in shaping the occurrence of suicide.

The role of suggestion in suicide has been clearly shown in Phillips's research on the effects of publicized suicides on national suicide rates. Suggestion and learning experiences also clearly play a role in the choice of method for suicide. The existence of famous suicide venues proves this, especially the differential use of the two major bridges in the San Francisco area. There is also good evidence that experience in youthful years with guns leads to a greater likelihood of their use for suicide. The research in Australia by Burvill, showing that immigrants switch to the Australian methods for suicide, also supports the social learning viewpoint.

Finally, the existence of high rates of suicidal behavior in the friends and relatives of suicidal people suggests the role of imitation and vicarious learning in determining suicidal behavior.

REFERENCES

Achte, K., & Lonnqvist, J.: Studies of psychiatric patients in Helsinki. *Proceedings of the 5th International Congress on Suicide Prevention*. Vienna: IASP, 1970.

Ashton, J., & Donnan, S.: Suicide by burning. *British Medical Journal*, 2:769-770, 1979.

Bandura, A.: *Social learning theory*. Englewood Cliffs: Prentice-Hall, 1977.

Bandura, A., & Walters, R.: *Adolescent aggression*. New York: Ronald, 1959.

Barraclough, B.: Suicide prevention, recurrent affective disorder and lithium. *British Journal of Psychiatry*, 121:391-392, 1972.

Barraclough, B., Shepherd, D., & Jennings, C.: Do newspaper reports of coroners' inquests incite people to commit suicide? *British Journal of Psychiatry*, 131:528-532, 1977.

Beck, A., Kovacs, M., & Weissman, A.: Hopelessness and suicidal behavior. *Journal of the American Medical Association*, 234:1146-1149, 1975.

Beck, A., Kovacs, M., & Weissman, A.: Assessment of suicidal intention. *Journal of Consulting and Clinical Psychology*, 47:343-352, 1979.

Beck, A., & Lester, D.: Components of depression in attempted suicides. *Journal of Psychology*, 85:257-260, 1973.

Beck, A., Weissman, A., & Kovacs, M.: Alcoholism, hopelessness and suicidal behavior. *Journal of Studies in Alcohol*, 37: 66-77, 1976.

Blumenthal, S., & Berger, L.: Suicide and newspapers. *American Journal of Psychiatry*, 130:468-471, 1973.

Bollen, K., & Phillips, D.: Suicidal motor vehicle fatalities in Detroit. *American Journal of Sociology*, 87:404-412, 1981.

Bollen, K., & Phillips, D.: Imitative suicides. *American Sociological Review*, 47:802-809, 1982.

Budner, S., & Kumler, F.: Correlates of suicidal ideation. Houston, American Association of Suicidology, 1973.

Burns, D.: *Feeling good*. New York: Morrow, 1980.

Burvill, P., McCall, M., Reid, T., & Stenhouse, N.: Methods of suicide in English and Welsh immigrants in Australia. *British Journal of Psychiatry*, 123:285-294, 1973.

Burvill, P., McCall, M., Woodings, T., & Stenhouse, N.: Comparison of suicide rates and methods in English, Scots and Irish immigrants in Australia. *Social Science & Medicine*, 17:705-708, 1983.

Burvill, P., Woodings, T., Stenhouse, N., & McCall, M.: Suicide during 1961-1970 migrants in Australia. *Psychological Medicine*, 12:295-308, 1982.

Buss, A., & Durkee, A.: An inventory for assessing different kinds of hostility. *Journal of Consulting Psychology*, 21:343-348, 1957.

Carr, E.: The motivation of self-injurious behavior. *Psychological Bulletin*, 84:800-816, 1977.

Christie, R.: Unpublished paper, Columbia University, 1967.

Church, I., & Phillips, J.: Suggestion and suicide by plastic bag asphyxia. *British Journal of Psychiatry*, 144:100-101, 1984.

Cohen, A.: *Delinquent boys*. Glencoe: Free Press, 1955.

Cohen, J.: *Behavior in uncertainty and its social consequences*. New York: Basic, 1964.

Corder, B., Page, P., & Corder, R.: Parental history, family communication and interaction patterns in adolescent suicide. *Family Therapy*, 1:285-290, 1974.

Crawford, J., & Willis, J.: Double suicide in psychiatric hospital patients. *British Journal of Psychiatry*, 112:1231-1235, 1966.

Coleman, L.: *Suicide clusters*. Boston: Faber & Faber, 1987.

Crosby, K., Rhee, J., & Holland, J.: Suicide by fire. *International Journal of Social Psychiatry*, 23:60-69, 1977.

DeCatanzaro, D.: *Suicide and self-damaging behavior*. New York: Academic Press, 1981.

Devries, A.: A potential suicide personality inventory. *Psychological Reports*, 18:731-738, 1966.

Diekstra, R.: A social learning theory approach to the prediction of suicidal behavior. *Proceedings of the 7th International Congress for Suicide Prevention*. Amsterdam: Swets & Zeitlinger BV, 1974.

Doroff, D.: Attempted and gestured suicide in adolescent girls. *Dissertation Abstracts*, 27B:2631, 1969.

Douglas, J.: *The social meanings of suicide*. Princeton: Princeton University Press, 1967.

Dublin, L.: *Suicide*. New York: Ronald, 1963.

Dublin, L., & Bunzel, B.: *To be or not to be*. New York: Harrison Smith & Robert Haas, 1933.

Durkheim, E.: *Suicide*. Glencoe: Free Press, 1951.

Ellis, A.: *Humanistic psychotherapy*. New York: Julian, 1973.

Ettlinger, R.: Suicide in a group of patients who had previously attempted suicide. *Acta Psychiatrica Scandinavia*, 40:364-378, 1964.

Eysenck, H.: *Crime and personality*. London: Paladin, 1970.

Farber, M.: *Theory of suicide*. New York: Funk & Wagnalls, 1968.

Farberow, N., & Shneidman, E.: *The cry for help*. New York: McGraw-Hill, 1961.

Ferracuti, F.: Suicide in a Catholic country. In E.S. Shneidman & N.L. Farberow (Eds.) *Clues to suicide*. New York: McGraw-Hill, 1957.

Ferster, C.: Positive reinforcement and behavioral deficits of autistic children. *Child Development*, 32:437-456, 1961.

Ferster, C.: Behavioral approaches to depression. In R.J. Friedman & M.M. Katz (Eds.) *The psychology of depression*. Washington, DC: Winston, 1974.

Finlay, S.: Suicide and self-injury in Leeds University students. *Proceedings of the 5th International Conference for Suicide Prevention*. Vienna: IASP, 1970.

Firth, R.: Suicide and risk-taking in Tikopia. *Psychiatry*, 24:1-17, 1961.

Frank, M.: Why people gamble. In D. Lester (Ed.) *Why people gamble*. Springfield: Thomas, 1979, 71-83.

Frederick, C., & Resnick, H.: How suicidal behaviors are learned. *American Journal of Psychotherapy*, 25:37-55, 1971.

Garfinkel, B., Froese, A., & Golombek, H.: Suicidal behavior in a pediatric population. *Proceedings of the 10th International Congress for Suicide Prevention*. Ottawa: IASP, 1979.

Gastil, R.: Homicide and a regional culture of violence. *American Sociological Review*, 36:412-427, 1971.

Gold, M.: Suicide, homicide, and the socialization of aggression. *American Journal of Sociology*, 63:651-661, 1958.

Graff, H., & Mallin, R.: The syndrome of the wrist-cutter. *American Journal of Psychiatry*, 124:36-42, 1967.

Greenwald, H.: *Direct decision therapy*. San Diego: EDITS, 1973.

Guze, S., & Robins, E.: Suicide and primary affective disorder. *British Journal of Psychiatry*, 117:437-438, 1970.

Hankoff, L.: An epidemic of attempted suicide. *Comprehensive Psychiatry*, 2:294-298, 1961.

Hauschild, T.: Suicidal population of a military psychiatric center. *Military Medicine*, 133:425-437, 1968.

Headley, L.: *Suicide in Asia and the Near East*. Berkeley: University of California, 1983.

Henderson, J.: Competence, threat, hope and self-destructive behavior. *Dissertation Abstracts International*, 33B:439, 1972.

Hendin, H.: *Suicide and Scandinavia.* New York: Doubleday, 1965.

Henry, A., & Short, J.: *Suicide and homicide.* Glencoe: Free Press, 1954.

Hill, O.: The association of childhood bereavement with suicide in depressive illnesses. *British Journal of Psychiatry,* 115:159-164, 1969.

Hirsh, J.: Methods and fashions of suicide. *Mental Hygiene,* 44:3-11, 1960.

Hoskin, J., Friedman, M., & Cawte, J.: A high incidence of suicide in a preliterate primitive society. *Psychiatry,* 32:200-210, 1969.

Jacobs, J.: *Adolescent suicide.* New York: Wiley, 1971.

Johnson, B.: Durkheim's one cause of suicide. *American Sociological Review,* 30:875-886, 1965.

Johnson, B.: *Marihuana users and drug subcultures.* New York: Wiley, 1973.

Johnson, G., & Hunt, G.: Suicidal behavior in bipolar manic-depressive patients and their families. *Comprehensive Psychiatry,* 20:159-164, 1979.

Kirch, M., & Lester, D.: Suicide from the Golden Gate Bridge. *Psychological Reports,* 59:1314, 1986a.

Kirch, M., & Lester, D.: Clusters of suicide. *Psychological Reports,* 59:1126, 1986b.

Kreitman, N., Smith, P., & Tan, E.: Attempted suicide in social networks. *British Journal of Preventive & Social Medicine,* 23:116-123, 1969.

Lambley, P., & Silbowitz, M.: Rotter's internal-external scale and prediction of suicide contemplators among students. *Psychological Reports,* 33:585-586, 1973.

Leonard, C.: *Understanding and preventing suicide.* Springfield: Thomas, 1967.

Lester, D.: Suicide, homicide, and the effects of socialization. *Journal of Personality & Social Psychology,* 5:466-468, 1967.

Lester, D.: Attempted suicide as a hostile act. *Journal of Psychology,* 68:243-248, 1968a.

Lester, D.: Punishment experiences and suicidal preoccupation. *Journal of Genetic Psychology,* 113:89-94, 1968b.

Lester, D.: Suicide and Machiavellianism. Unpublished, Suicide Prevention & Crisis Service, 1970.

Lester, D.: *Why people kill themselves.* Springfield: Thomas, 1972.

Lester, D.: The myth of suicide prevention. *Comprehensive Psychiatry,* 13:555-560, 1972a.

Lester, D.: Self-mutilating behavior. *Psychological Bulletin,* 78:119-128, 1972b.

Lester, D.: Migration and suicide. *Medical Journal of Australia,* 1:941-942, 1972c.

Lester, D.: Sex differences in suicidal behavior. In E. Gomberg & V. Franks (Eds.) *Gender and disordered behavior.* New York: Brunner/Mazel, 1979.

Lester, D.: *Why people kill themselves.* Springfield: Thomas, 1983.

Lester, D.: Societal approval of suicide. *Australian & New Zealand Journal of Psychiatry,* 17:293, 1983a.

Lester, D.: A subcultural theory of teenage suicide. *Adolescence,* 22:317-320, 1987.

Lester, D., & Beck, A.: Suicidal intent, medical lethality of the suicide attempt, and components of depression. *Journal of Clinical Psychology,* 31:11-12, 1975.

Lester, D., & Beck, A.: Early loss as a possible sensitizer to later loss in attempted suicides. *Psychological Reports,* 39:121-122, 1976.

Lester, D., & Beck, A.: Suicidal wishes and depression in suicidal ideators. *Journal of Clinical Psychology,* 33:92-94, 1977.

Lester, D., Beck, A.T., & Narrett, S.: Suicidal intent in successive suicidal actions. *Psychological Reports*, 43:110, 1978.

Lester, D., & Brockopp, G.: Niagara Falls suicide. *Journal of the American Medical Association*, 215:797-798, 1971.

Lester, G., & Lester, D.: *Suicide: the gamble with death*. Englewood Cliffs: Prentice-Hall, 1971.

Levenson, M.: Cognitive and perceptual factors in suicidal individuals. *Dissertation Abstracts International*, 33B:5521, 1973.

Lewinsohn, P.: A behavioral approach to depression. In R.J. Friedman & M.M. Katz (Eds.) *The psychology of depression*. New York: Halstead, 1974.

Lewinsohn, P., & Graf, M.: Pleasant activities and depression. *Journal of Consulting and Clinical Psychology*, 41:261-268, 1973.

Linehan, M.: Suicide and attempted suicide. *Perceptual & Motor Skills*, 37:31-34, 1973.

Maddison, D., & Mackey, K.: Suicide. *British Journal of Psychiatry*, 112:693-703, 1966.

Marks, A., & Abernathy, T.: Toward a sociocultural perspective on means of self-destruction. *Life-Threatening Behavior*, 4:3-17, 1974.

Marks, A., & Stokes, C.: Socialization, firearms and suicide. *Social Problems*, 23:622-629, 1976.

McHugh, P., & Goodell, H.: Suicidal behavior. *Archives of General Psychiatry*, 25:456-464, 1971.

Meerloo, J.: *Suicide and mass suicide*. New York: Grune & Stratton, 1962.

Menninger, K.: *Man against himself*. New York: Harcourt Brace & World, 1938.

Minkoff, K., Bergman, E., Beck, A., & Beck, R.: Hopelessness, depression and attempted suicide. *American Journal of Psychiatry*, 130:455-459, 1973.

Mintz, J., O'Brien, C., Woody, C., & Beck, A.: Depression in treated narcotic addicts, ex-addicts, nonaddicts and suicide attempters. *American Journal of Drug and Alcohol Abuse*, 6:385-396, 1979.

Morselli, H.: *Suicide*. New York: Appleton, 1882.

Motto, J.: Suicide and suggestibility. *American Journal of Psychiatry*, 124:252-256, 1967.

Motto, J.: Newspaper influence on suicide. *Archives of General Psychiatry*, 23:143-148, 1970.

Murphy, G., Wetzel, R., Swallow, C., & McClure, J.: Who calls the suicide prevention center? *American Journal of Psychiatry*, 126:314-324, 1969.

Neuringer, C.: Rigid thinking in suicidal individuals. *Journal of Consulting Psychology*, 28:54-58, 1964.

Niemi, T.: The time-space distance of suicides committed in the lock-up in Finland in 1963-1967. *Psychiatria Fennica*, 1975:267-270, 1975.

Pallis, D., & Sainsbury, P.: The value of assessing intent in attempted suicide. *Psychological Medicine*, 6:487-492, 1976.

Phares, E.: *Locus of control in personality*. Morristown: Silver Burdett, 1976.

Phillips, D.: The influences of suggestion on suicide. *American Sociological Review*, 39:340-354.

Phillips, D.: Motor vehicle fatalities increase just after publicized suicide stories. *Science*, 196:1464-1466, 1977.

Phillips, D.: Airplane accidents fatalities increase just after newspaper stories about murder and suicide. *Science*, 201:748-750, 1978.

Phillips, D.: Suicide, motor vehicle fatalities and the mass media. *American Journal of Sociology*, 84:1150-1174, 1979.

Phillips, D.: The impact of fictional television stories on U.S. adult fatalities. *American Journal of Sociology*, 87:1340-1359, 1982.

Pokorny, A.: Characteristics of 44 patients who subsequently committed suicide. *Archives of General Psychiatry*, 2:314-323, 1960.

Pokorny, A.: Suicide rates in various psychiatric disorders. *Journal of Nervous and Mental Disease*, 139:499-506, 1964.

Pollack, B.: A study of the problem of suicide. *Psychiatric Quarterly*, 12:306-330, 1938.

Rachman, S., & Hodgson, R.: Experimentally induced "sexual fetishism." *Psychological Record*, 18:25-27, 1968.

Richman, J.: *Family therapy for suicidal people.* New York: Springer, 1986.

Robins, L., West, P., & Murphy, G.: The high rate of suicide in older white men. *Social Psychiatry*, 12:1-20, 1977.

Rorsman, B.: Suicide in psychiatric patients. *Social Psychiatry*, 8:55-66, 1973.

Rosen, D.: The serious suicide attempt. *American Journal of Psychiatry*, 127:764-770, 1970.

Rotter, J.: Generalized expectancies for internal versus external reinforcement. *Psychological Monographs*, 80:#1, 1966.

Sainsbury, P., & Barraclough, B.: Differences between suicide rates. *Nature*, 220:1252, 1968.

Seiden, R.: Suicide behavior contagion on a college campus. *Proceedings of the 4th International Congress for Suicide Prevention.* Los Angeles: Delmar, 1968.

Seiden, R., & Spence, N.: A tale of two bridges. *Omega*, 3:201-209, 1983-1984.

Seligman, M.: Depression and learned helplessness. In R.J. Friedman & M. Katz (Eds.) *The psychology of depression.* New York: Halstead, 1974.

Selkin, J.: Probe of suicides points way to prevention. *Network News*, #4:14, 1986.

Sifneos, P.: Manipulative suicide. *Psychiatric Quarterly*, 40:525-537, 1966.

Silver, M., Bohnert, M., & Beck, A.: Relation of depression of attempted suicides and seriousness of intent. *Archives of General Psychiatry*, 25:573-576, 1971.

Sletten, I., Evenson, R., & Brown, M.: Some results from an automated statewide comparison among attempted, committed and nonsuicidal patients. *Life-Threatening Behavior*, 3:191-197, 1973.

Steer, R., Beck, A., Garrison, B., & Lester, D.: Eventual suicide and suicidal intent in interrupted and uninterrupted attempters. *Suicide & Life-Threatening Behavior*, 1988.

Temoche, A., Pugh, T., & MacMahon, B.: Suicide rates among current and former mental institution patients. *Journal of Nervous and Mental Disease*, 138:124-130, 1964.

Toman, W.: *An introduction to the psychoanalytic theory of motivation.* New York: Pergamon, 1960.

Tucker, G., & Reinhardt, R.: *Suicide attempts*, U.S. Naval Aerospace Medical Institute, 1966.

Waldstein, E.: *Der Selbstmord in der Schweiz.* Basle: Philographischer Verlag, 1934.

Weissman, A., Beck, A., & Kovacs, M.: Drug abuse, hopelessness and suicidal behavior. *International Journal of Addictions*, 14:451-464, 1979.

Winokur, G., Morrison, J., Clancy, J., & Crow, R.: The Iowa 500. *Comprehensive Psychiatry*, 14:99-106, 1973.

Wolfgang, M., & Ferracuti, F.: *The subculture of violence.* New York: Tavistock, 1969.

Woodruff, R., Clayton, P., & Guze, S.: Suicide attempts and psychiatric diagnosis. *Diseases of the Nervous System*, 33:617-621, 1972.

Chapter 4

GEORGE KELLY'S
PERSONAL CONSTRUCT THEORY

GEORGE KELLY (1955) proposed a theory of the structure of the mind based upon cognitive processes (thinking). His basic idea was that we attempt to interpret and make sense of the events that we experience. Our psychological processes and our behaviors are determined by the way in which we anticipate events (or in Kelly's terms, how we construe events).

At the highest level of abstraction, we may be seen as having a theory of the world (a *construction system*). Usually, we seek to extend and refine our construction system. We try to develop a construction system that applies to more and more of the experiences that we encounter, and we try to make it more accurate in the predictions to which it leads us.

Clearly, the theory is a growth-oriented theory in which we become more skilled in making sense of the world in which we live. For Kelly, the model for human behavior is the theoretical scientist who proposes a theory of some phenomenon and then tries to modify the theory to account for all the new data that empirical scientists accumulate about the phenomenon.

As we continue to exist, therefore, we experience more and more, and so our construction system changes and becomes a more accurate predictor for future events. However, it is possible to have inconsistencies and incompatibilities in our construction system. The view of the world we have when we are depressed is often quite different from that which we have when we are happy. When we use only one part of our construction to interpret today's events, we are said to have *suspended* the remaining inconsistent parts.

69

The Basic Concepts

Construction systems are composed of *constructs*, concepts which we apply to events when we experience them. Constructs are bipolar and dichotomous. When we construe an event we decide that it is *either* this *or* that. Each of us has idiosyncratic constructs. For example, at graduate school, I had a professor who classified people on the basis of their ability as either intelligent or handicapped. Kelly stressed that it was important to find out how both ends of the construct were labelled by the person since they may not use the same label as we would. I might use stupid as the opposite of intelligent, but my professor used handicapped.

The poles of the construct may be used frequently and consciously, in which case the pole is said to be *emergent*; it may be *implicit*, rarely used and not obvious to the person; or it may be *submerged*, never used and unconscious.

Types of Constructs

Kelly was not concerned with identifying particular constructs that are commonly used. Rather he defined various properties of constructs. Constructs have a *range of convenience*, a set of events or objects to which they are typically applied. Constructs may be *preverbal* because we developed them before we had good language skills to symbolize them. Constructs may be *propositional*, that is, classification of an event with one construct does not imply anything about how it will be classified in other constructs, or the opposite, *constellatory*. Constellatory thinking is illustrated by sexist and racist ideas. If you meet a man about whom you know nothing and say, "This is a man; therefore he is rational, insensitive, cold, brutal and oppresses women," you are construing in a constellatory manner.

Constructs may be applicable to your conception of your innermost self, in which case they are called *core* constructs; or only tangentially relevant to your sense of self, in which case they are called *peripheral* constructs. In general, psychotherapy deals with your core constructs while education deals with your peripheral constructs.

Construction Systems

Construction systems, or parts of them, may be *tight* or *loose*. In tight construing, your theory of the world makes clear unambiguous predictions about what will happen. In loose construing, your theory does not make clear predictions. Daydreams employ tight thinking in general, while dreams employ loose thinking. Creative thinking is frequently loose but, in order to communicate creative ideas to others, tightening of the ideas must occur. (Einstein's early musing on his innovative ideas in physics might well have passed through a loose period, but to publish the ideas for others to read and use required tightening of them.)

The Perceptual Field

The *perceptual field* is what we experience. It is our subjective perception of the external world. If we explore this external world and seek to gain new experiences, we are said to be *dilating*. On the other hand, if we withdraw from new experiences and retreat into a more well-known world, we are said to be *constricting*.

Reconceptualization of Familiar Concepts

In addition to defining a new set of concepts, Kelly also considered that the traditional meaning of some familiar terms could be improved, in particular by looking at their implications from the person's point of view and from a personal construct perspective.

Threat

Threat is when you anticipate that you are about to experience some events that will necessitate a substantial change in your core constructs. This will involve a reconceptualization of who you really are and will involve developing a new set of constructs. We commonly call this an identity crisis.

Fear is what you experience when you anticipate that there will be a change in your peripheral constructs, clearly not as major a process as threat.

Anxiety

Anxiety is an awareness that your construction system does not make adequate predictions for the events which you are experiencing. You cannot construe these events. There are various reasons for this. For example, it may be that you have never experienced these types of events before, and your construction system does not apply to them. Or that the experiences are occuring too fast for you to assimilate them. Or that the experiences may have inherent contradictions and inconsistencies so that they cannot be assimilated.

Aggression

Aggression involves the active elaboration of your perceptual field. You go out and seek experiences, often in those areas which cause you anxiety (and which, therefore, you cannot construe accurately). The opposite to aggression is *passivity*.

Hostility

When you are confronted with evidence that shows that your construction system is incorrect or inadequate in its predictions, you can seek to modify your construction system so that it becomes more adequate. If instead, you seek to distort the evidence so that it remains consistent with your old construction system, you are said to be *hostile*.

The use of psychoanalytic defense mechanisms (which involve the distortion of evidence) is a hostile act. Hostility may also involve extorting evidence from the environment that is consistent with your old construction system. Most of the strategies discribed by Leon Festinger (1957) in his theory of cognitive dissonance are hostile. The smoker who, for example, does not notice the warning on the package saying that smoking is hazardous to his health or who refuses to believe that smoking causes lung cancer is behaving in a hostile fashion.

Kelly on Suicide

Kelly (1961) was asked to write specifically on the determinants of suicide. He first stressed that suicide, like most of the other behaviors of a person, was an attempt to validate one's life. It will be consistent with the person's construct system and serve to reinforce the particular theory that the person has adopted.

Secondly, he noted that suicide will occur when the outcome of events is so obvious (and we might add anticipated to be extremely unpleasant) that there is no point in waiting around for them. Kelly noted the similarity of this idea to fatalism. If the future is anticipated to be unpleasant and painful, then the person will experience hopelessness. Neimeyer (1984) has speculated that suicidal acts committed in this state will be deliberate, well planned and lethal.

Suicide will also occur when everything seems so unpredictable that the only definite action is to leave the scene completely. This will be a condition of extreme anxiety. Neimeyer suggested that suicidal actions committed in this state will be impulsive, poorly planned and less lethal.

Kelly noted that suicide, like depression, was an act of extreme constriction. In constriction, the person shrinks his world to a manageable size. While the depressed person constricts his world by withdrawing from some activity, suicide involves an extreme degree of constriction.

Suicide as a Hostile Act

Lester (1968) suggested that some forms of suicide may be seen as hostile acts. Often suicide, especially attempts at suicide, are ways of extorting evidence from the world to conform to some particular viewpoint that the suicidal person has.

If a lover is leaving, the attempt at suicide may be motivated by a desire to extort confirmation that the departing lover really does love you and will not leave after all. Alternatively, but more rarely and less obviously, the attempt may be a way of extorting rejection from others to confirm a belief on the part of the suicidal person that people cannot be trusted and that the world is a rejecting place.

In his research, Lester (1969) found that attempted suicides expressed more resentment than nonsuicidal people. The resentment was shown to be directed toward those upon whom the suicidal person was dependent. The suicidal person resented the world and felt that he had been treated unjustly. Lester argued that his suicidal attempts may have been planned to give others a chance to reject him, thereby validating his resentment against the world. By his suicidal actions, he risks being rejected by those who are important to him. (The suicidal person often makes it more difficult for his parents, his peers, and his wife or girlfriend to love him and accept him.)

The suicide attempt may also serve to validate other beliefs. The suicidal person often experiences feelings of worthlessness and depression. By risking rejection through his suicidal behavior, he can seek a validation of his worthlessness and a demonstration that his is not worth caring about.

Lester's ideas differed from the more traditional view of the suicidal person, which sees the aim of the suicide attempt to lie in the extortion of love and attention from others, though this is still hostile behavior in Kelly's theory. These two differing views suggest the possibility of conflict in the suicidal individual, a conflict between the seeking of love and the seeking of rejection. We might speculate that this conflict is a feature which differentiates individuals who attempt suicide from those who successfully kill themselves. The successful suicide may not be seeking rejection, but rather love and attention. Although he will not be able to receive this love and attention, the suicidal person often acts as if he will be around to savor it. Shneidman and Farberow (1957) have called this kind of thinking *catalogic*.

Leenaars's Description of Kelly's Views

Leenaars (1988) has endeavored to specify the views of Kelly on suicide so that he could examine the content of suicide notes to explore whether such notes illustrated Kelly's views. Leenaars found ten basic ideas:

1. Suicide is an attempt to make sense out of whatever has happened to the person.
2. The person is killing himself because his worst expectations are coming true.
3. The suicidal person's expectations/anticipations about himself, others and the world are not coming true.
4. The suicidal person is expecting less and less for himself, others and the world.
5. The suicidal person feels helpless in understanding an unpredictable and senseless world.
6. The suicidal person is aware of events that don't make adequate sense to him.
7. The suicidal person needs to change himself in order to handle forthcoming events in a way that seems to be impossible to him.
8. The suicidal person has been trying or is trying to make people or events fit with what he expects is the right thing.
9. The suicidal person does not seem to fit into or be able to do what other people expect of him.
10. The suicidal person is killing himself because he sees no alternative to this action and he sees the suicide as giving him some meaning in life.

Leenaars found that none of these themes differentiated genuine from simulated suicide notes and, furthermore, none of them occurred in at least two-thirds of the genuine suicide notes.

Empirical Evidence for Kelly's Ideas

What evidence is there for the validity of Kelly's ideas about suicide? Very little research on suicide has been conducted within the framework of Kelly's theory. Furthermore, since his theory focusses on cognitive processes and since very little general research has been carried on the cognitive processes of suicidal people, there is not much empirical evidence available that is pertinent to Kelly's ideas. However, some research has relevance for the theory.

General Research on Thinking in Suicidal People

Neuringer has carried out a series of studies to investigate the thought processes of the suicidal individual. In his first study (Neuringer, 1961), he investigated whether suicidal people have a tendency to think in terms of absolute value dichotomies. This tendency would result in the individual polarizing his evaluations into extreme values, such as good versus bad or right versus wrong.

To investigate dichotomous thinking, Neuringer used the Semantic Differential in which the subject has to rate different concepts (such as democracy, love, life, etc.) on different scales (such as good-bad, clean-dirty, happy-sad, etc.). Each concept can be judged on a scale with three degrees of agreement (for example, very bad, moderately bad, and mildly bad). Twelve concepts were organized into pairs (life-death, honor-shame, etc.) and the difference in the ratings of these paired concepts over the scales of judgment was used to measure the tendency to evaluate dichotomously. Neuringer compared male suicide attempters, psychosomatic patients and normal people. Neuringer found that both the suicidal and psychosomatic patients made significantly more extreme judgments than normal people. The suicidal individuals did not differ from the psychosomatic patients, and so dichotomous thinking appeared to be characteristic of all disturbed patients and not unique to suicidal individuals.

In a re-analysis of the data from this study including more of the rating scales, Neuringer (1967) found that the suicidal individuals did show more dichotomous thinking than the psychosomatic patients.

Neuringer (1964) investigated rigid thinking in these same patients, using an attitude scale and a problem-solving task. On both tests, the suicidal patients behaved significantly more rigidly than the psychosomatic patients and the normal people. Patsiokas, et al. (1979) also found suicidal people to be more rigid as compared to nonsuicidal psychiatric patients.

Later Neuringer (1979a, 1979b; Neuringer and Lettieri, 1971) found that suicidal people rated the concepts of life and death more extremely than comparison patients and that suicidal people with a higher risk of suicide rated the concepts more extremely than suicidal individuals with a lower degree of risk.

Kelly's notion of the basic cognitive elements in the mind is that they are bipolar concepts. Whether this is indeed true or not, the research of Neuringer shows that suicidal people certainly do seem to construe concepts relevant to living and dying more dichotomously than nonsuicidal individuals.

In line with this finding, Osgood and Walker (1959) found that genuine suicide notes contained more "allness" terms (such as always and never) than simulated suicide notes.

Secondly, one of the prerequisites of hostility is that the individual must be reluctant to change and modify their construction system. This is not the same as simple measures of rigidity as measured by standard psychological tests. However, the research showing that suicidal people are more rigid than nonsuicidal people is consistent with the conceptualization of suicidal people as hostile.

Constriction

Neimeyer (1984) reviewed research relative to Kelly's notion that the suicidal person constricts as a general strategy. Landfield (1976) tried to measure constriction using the REP test by noting whether the individual was unable to classify a significant other using the constructs identified on the REP test and whether the individual used concrete constructs. He found that suicide attempters did indeed appear to be more constricted on these measures.

Neimeyer also felt that research showing that genuine suicide notes contained more concern with minor details, trivia and neutral statements than simulated notes (Shneidman and Farberow, 1957) as showing constriction.

However, both of these studies focus on the construction system of the suicidal individual. Constriction refers rather to the perceptual field. A constricted individual restricts the inflow of information into his mind. Thus, the studies reviewed by Neimeyer do not really explore constriction.

There are no studies specifically designed to explore Kelly's notion of constriction of the perceptual field. But some research is pertinent to the issue. For example, the unequivocal research showing that suicide is most closely associated with the psychiatric syndrome of depression (for example, see Temoche, et al. [1964]) supports the notion of suicide as an act of a constricting individual since depression (with symptoms of motor retardation, apathy and loss of interest in the world) is a constricting behavior.

Several researchers have found that suicidal people are more present-oriented and have less future time perspective (Greaves, 1971; Neuringer, et al., 1971; Yufit and Benzies, 1973). This would be consistent with constriction, since the suicidal people would be restricting thoughts of the future from intrusion into their consciousness.

Several studies have also reported that suicides are more socially isolated than nonsuicidal people. For example, Bock and Webber (1972) found that the suicide rate in the elderly was higher if they were unmarried, had few relatives around and belonged to few organizations. Humphrey, et al. (1971) found that suicide attempters were less likely to be married and more residentially mobile. They had weaker family ties and fewer interactions with relatives. They argued with friends (though interacting with them more) and preferred to be alone. Nelson, et al. (1977) also found that attempted suicides were less socially involved than nonsuicidal psychiatric patients.

However, not all research supports this social withdrawal. Finlay (1970) and Greth (1973) found suicidal and nonsuicidal college students to have similar levels of involvement in organizations and college activities, though playing team sports less often.

This social withdrawal may be a result of the depression and suicidal involvement and it may be a contributing cause (a "vicious" cycle). In Kelly's theory, the constriction is part of the suicidal life-style, especially in the period prior to the suicidal action.

System Disorganization and Anxiety

Kelly hypothesized, as we have seen, that suicide may be a response to the anxiety associated with the collapse of the personal construct system. Landfield (1976) sought to explore system disorganization in suicidal people by examining how many clusters of constructs they used in responding to the REP test. Landfield found, as predicted, that suicide attempters had more disorganized construction systems than comparison patients.

(Lester [1971] sought to examine this hypothesis, but he used the RES test which is not a suitable technique for testing the hypothesis.)

Fatalistic Depression

The presence of fatalistic depression in suicides is best documented by the research of Aaron Beck and his associates on hopelessness in suicidal patients. Beck, et al. (1975, 1979) found that a measure of hopelessness, a cognitive component of the depression syndrome, was more strongly correlated with suicidal intent in suicide attempters and with the degree of suicidal ideation in suicidal ideators. Lester, et al. (1979) found that hopelessness scores increased from those making gestures to those making serious attempts and that those subsequently completing suicide were among the most hopeless at the time of their initial suicide attempt.

Not every investigator finds that hopelessness is a stronger predictor of suicidal intent than general depression (for example, Pokorny, et al., 1975), but all agree that hopelessness predicts suicidal intent.

Impulsive Construing

In construing, Kelly noted that typically people construe propositionally for a while before preempting and deciding how the situation may best be understood. The impulsive person has a very brief propositional phase while the obsessive person has too long a propositional phase.

It has commonly been noted that suicidal people are often impulsive. Corder, et al. (1974), for example, reported that adolescent suicidal attempters were more impulsive and had a higher activity level than controls. More recent research has compared impulsive and nonimpulsive attempters. Williams, et al. (1977) found, for example, that impulsive attempters were more likely to have a history of suicide attempts and had the means for attempting suicide more readily available.

Using Megargee's (1966) concepts of overcontrol and undercontrol, Lester and Wright (1973) speculated that suicide attempters may be undercontrolled (impulsive in Kelly's terminology), while completed suicides may be overcontrolled (constricted emotionally in Kelly's terminology).

Negative Self-Construing

Neimeyer (1984) notes that negative self-construing may also be an important accompaniment of suicidal preoccupation. All research confirms this (Neuringer, 1974; Wentz, 1976; Wetzel, 1976). Kaplan and Pokorny (1976) found that low self-esteem also predicted *subsequent* suicidal thoughts, threats and attempts in seventh-grade children.

Neimeyer (1984) summarized the interaction of self-esteem and depression in suicidal people in this way. At mild levels of depression, the self-schema begins to lose some of its organization as it begins to assimilate negative as well as positive information about the self. This continues until, at moderate levels of depression, inconsistent self-construing dominates the system. As the depression deepens, a stable and consistent negative self-schema emerges. The degree of negative self-construing appears to vary with the intensity of symptoms, while other traits such as polarized construing may be stable personality traits of the suicidal person.

Discussion

It can be seen that several lines of research support ideas about suicide that can be derived from Kelly's theory of personal constructs. Constriction of the perceptual field, disorganization of the construction system, anticipatory failure of the predictive system, impulsive construing, negative self-construing, polarized construing and hostility all may characterize the suicidal individual. In addition, several case studies of suicidal people have appeared with a personal construct theory perspective (Ryle, 1967). Thus, the personal construct perspective may prove to be a stimulant for innovative research into suicide.

REFERENCES

Beck, A., Kovacs, M., & Weissman, A.: Hopelessness and suicidal behavior. *Journal of the American Medical Association*, 234:1146-1149, 1975.

Beck, A., Kovacs, M., & Weissman, A.: Assessment of suicidal intention. *Journal of Consulting & Clinical Psychology*, 47:343-352, 1979.

Bock, E., & Webber, I.: Social status and relational system of elderly suicides. *Life-Threatening Behavior*, 2:145-159, 1972.

Corder, B., Shorr, W., & Corder, R.: A study of social and psychological characteristics of adolescent suicide attempters in an urban disadvantaged area. *Adolescence*, 9:1-6, 1974.

Festinger, L.: *A theory of cognitive dissonance*. Palo Alto: Stanford University Press, 1957.

Finlay, S.: Suicide and self-injury in Leeds University students. *Proceedings of the 5th International Congress for Suicide Prevention*. Vienna: IASP, 1970.

Greaves, G.: Temporal orientation in suicidal patients. *Perceptual & Motor Skills*, 33:1020, 1971.

Greth, D.: Anomie, suicidal ideation and student ecology in a student population. *Dissertation Abstracts International*, 33B:3305, 1973.

Humphrey, J., Niswander, D., & Casey, T.: A comparison of suicide thinkers and attempters. *Diseases of the Nervous System*, 32:825-830, 1971.

Kaplan, H., & Pokorny, A.: Self-derogation and suicide. *Social Science & Medicine*, 10:113-121, 1976.

Kelly, G.: *The psychology of personal constructs*. New York: Norton, 1955.

Kelly, G.: Suicide. In N. Faberow & E. Shneidman (Eds.) *The cry for help*. New York: McGraw-Hill, 1967.

Landfield, A.: A personal construct approach to suicidal behavior. In P. Slater (Ed.) *Explorations of intrapersonal space*. New York: Wiley, 1976.

Leenaars, A.A.: *Suicide notes*. New York: Human Sciences, 1988.

Lester, D.: Attempted suicide as a hostile act. *Journal of Psychology*, 68:243-248, 1968.

Lester, D.: Resentment and dependency in the suicidal individual. *Journal of General Psychology*, 81:137-145, 1969.

Lester, D.: Cognitive complexity of the suicidal individual. *Psychological Reports*, 28:158, 1971.

Lester, D., Beck, A., & Mitchell, B.: Extrapolation from attempted suicide to completed suicide. *Journal of Abnormal Psychology*, 88, 78-80, 1970.

Lester, D., & Wright, T.: Suicide and overcontrol. *Psychological Reports*, 32:1278, 1973.

Megargee, E.: Undercontrolled and overcontrolled personality types in extreme antisocial aggression. *Psychological Monographs*, 80:#3, 1966.

Neimeyer, R.: Toward a personal construct conceptualization of depression and suicide. In F. Epting and R. Neimeyer (Eds.) *Personal meanings of death*. Washington: Hemisphere, 1984.

Nelson, V., Nielsen, E., & Chicketts, K.: Interpersonal attributes of suicidal individuals. *Psychological Reports*, 40:983-989, 1977.

Neuringer, C.: Self and other-appraisals by suicidal, psychosomatic and normal hospital patients. *Journal of Consulting and Clinical Psychology*, 42:306, 1974.

Neuringer, C.: Relationship between life and death among individuals of varying levels of suicidality. *Journal of Consulting and Clinical Psychology*, 47:407-408, 1979a.

Neuringer, C.: The semantic perception of life, death and suicide. *Journal of Clinical Psychology*, 35:255-258, 1979b.

Neuringer, C., Levenson, M., & Kaplan, J.: Phenomenological time flow in suicidal, geriatric and normal individuals. *Omega*, 2:247-251, 1971.

Neuringer, C., & Lettieri, D.: Cognition, attitude and affect in suicidal individuals. *Life-Threatening Behavior*, 1:106-124, 1971.

Osgood, C., & Walker, E.: Motivation and language behavior. *Journal of Abnormal & Social Psychology*, 59: 58-67, 1959.

Patsiokas, A., Clum, G., & Luscomb, R.: Cognitive characteristics of suicide attempters. *Journal of Consulting and Clinical Psychology*, 47:478-484, 1979.

Pokorny, A., Kaplan, H., & Tsai, S.: Hopelessness and attempted suicide. *American Journal of Psychiatry*, 132:954-956, 1975.

Ryle, A.: A repertory grid study of the meaning and consequences of a suicidal act. *British Journal of Psychiatry*, 113:1393-1403, 1967.

Shneidman, E., & Farberow, N.: The logic of suicide. In E. Shneidman & N. Farberow (Eds.) *Clues to suicide*. New York: McGraw-Hill, 1957.

Temoche, A., Pugh, T., & MacMahon, B.: Suicide rates among current and former mental institution patients. *Journal of Nervous & Mental Disease*, 138:124-130, 1964.

Wenz, F.: Self-evaluation and suicide potential. *Psychological Reports*, 39:289-290, 1976.

Wetzel, R.: Semantic differential ratings of concepts and suicide intent. *Journal of Clinical Psychology*, 32:4-13, 1976.

Williams, C., Sale, I., & Wignell, A.: Correlates of impulsive suicidal behavior. *New Zealand Medical Journal*, 85:323-325, 1977.

Yufit, R., & Benzies, B.: Assessing suicidal potential by time perspective. *Life-Threatening Behavior*, 3:270-282, 1973.

Chapter 5

ALFRED ADLER'S
INDIVIDUAL PSYCHOLOGY

INDIVIDUAL PSYCHOLOGY refers to the body of ideas developed by Alfred Adler. Adler's ideas were initially stimulated by Freud's psychoanalytic theory, but Adler soon began to place less emphasis upon the sources of motivation described by Freud in favor of social interest.

Social interest for Adler was an innate motivation. People want to relate to others, they engage in cooperative social activities, and they place the welfare of others above their personal and selfish interest. This motivation can be helped or hindered by the experiences of the child in his family and in his society.

Adler considered another basic drive in humans to be a striving for superiority. Although he first thought of this drive as one for aggression and power, he modified his later conception to that of superiority, by which he meant something like self-actualization, the perfect completion of one's style of life.

Adler felt that each personality was unique and could be characterized by its own life style. A person's life style is the system principle which shapes all of his psychological processes and behavior. This life style was formed very early in life, after which experiences were assimilated according to this life style. Organizing all of this is the creative self, a personal and subjective system which interprets and makes meaningful all of the person's experiences. The creative self seeks out and creates experiences that will help the person fulfill his life style. In particular, the creative self creates expectations for the future which guide the person. These expectations may be grounded in reality, but they may be fictitious, and Adler called this concept *fictional finalism*.

Adler's emphasis on life style and the creative self led him to place more importance on the conscious mind than either Freud or Jung had.

From a pathological point of view, people often have physiological and psychological weaknesses. These lead to feelings of inferiority and efforts to overcome these inferiorities by compensation. The stutterer becomes an orator, the sexually impotent man a Don Juan.

Psychological Disorder and Suicide

In his discussion of suicide from an Adlerian point of view, Ansbacher (1961, 1969) first noted that deficiency in social interest is a common factor in all disturbed people (neurotics, psychotics, addicts and criminals). Social interest involves the understanding and acceptance of the social inter-relatedness of the individual human life, the capacity to empathize with others, and to live in harmony with others and with the universe.

The suicide too is deficient in social interest. Often the suicide gives little or no thought to the effect of his death on others. He is pursuing selfish motives in his action. In this respect, clearly, Adler's notion of the suicide is similar to Durkheim's (1951) concept of *anomic* and *egoistic* suicide in which the individual lacks regulation by the society and integration into the society respectively.

This deficiency in social interest has its roots in childhood, where we typically find that the parents either hated and rejected the child or pampered him. This leads to a self-centered life style and a striving for personal success. Those with a pampered life style will tend to lean on others and demand that others satisfy their desires. When this fails to happen, they feel anger toward these other people, and Adler was aware that suicide is often an act of aggression against those others.

Ansbacher noted also that suicidal people will have developed feelings of inferiority and low self-esteem. In compensation, they seek to achieve great importance. They are ambitious and vain. Suicide gives such a person mastery over death. Ernest Hemingway's life and suicide perhaps is a good example of this.

The anger felt by the suicide toward others characterizes his whole life style. He often tries to hurt others by injuring himself, in actuality and in fantasy. Suicide is then but another example of reproach and revenge in this life style. Adler noted that suicidal people often try to manipulate others by sadness and suffering. They have fantasies of sickness and death, especially when they experience even minor stress.

What differentiates the suicide from anxiety neurotics and schizophrenics, and to a lesser extent from nonsuicidal depressed people and obsessive compulsives, is that they have a high degree of activity.[1]

Leenaars's Formulation of Adler's Ideas on Suicide

Leenaars (1988) identified ten components to Adler's ideas on suicide:

1. The individual is suffering from a particularly deep-seated feeling of inferiority, and he appears to be attempting to escape from the recognition of this inferiority feeling.
2. The individual has a lack of social interest.
3. The person desires a feeling of personal satisfaction, enhances his self, and achieves a heightened feeling of superiority without contributing to the welfare of the general community and is rather likely to disturb it by hurting or injuring some other person.
4. The person considers himself intelligent in the way he convinces himself of his personal superiority.
5. The person appears to have arrived at the end of his limited social interest and sees his suicide as a solution to an urgent problem or the injustices of life.
6. The person considers himself too weak to overcome his personal difficulties and therefore rejects everything with one action in order to escape the feeling of inferiority and to behave intelligently.
7. The person enhances his esteem by disparaging other people or by becoming lord over life and death.
8. Childhood problems (such as excessive hurt feelings or poor adjustment to loss or defeat) are likely to be the predisposing factors in the person's reaction to the current situation.
9. The unconscious mind of the person has created a situation in which death is desired, partly to attack or hurt someone else, or as an act of revenge toward someone who has injured him.
10. The person's aggression is turned inward. Themes of humility, submission and devotion, subordination, flagellation or masochism are present.

Leenaars compared the frequencies of these themes in samples of genuine and simulated suicide notes and found no differences. However, themes 5, 6, 9 and 10 were present in at least two-thirds of the genuine suicide notes.

---

[1]Ansbacher (1970) has discussed the suicide of Marilyn Monroe from an Adlerian perspective.

Research Related to Adler's Ideas

Childhood Experiences

Individual psychology would demand that we examine the childhoods of suicidal people to find the incidence of pampering and, to a lesser extent, abuse and neglect. However, researchers have not typically examined childhoods for these experiences.

Those interested in Adler's ideas have, however, stimulated a great deal of research on the effects of birth order, and this has been studied in suicidal individuals. Lester (1987) summarized all of the studies conducted on this topic and drew the following conclusions: there was an excess of first and middle borns in completed suicides and an excess of middle and last-borns among attempted suicides. The excess of last-borns (typically those most likely to be pampered) among attempted suicides suggests that Adler's analysis of suicides may be most pertinent to the suicide attempter.

Thinking Styles

Neuringer (1974) noted that Adler's description of the neurotic style of thinking included schematizing, excessive abstraction and rigidity. Neuringer reviewed his own research on the thinking of the suicidal individual, which has been summarized here in Chapter 4 on George Kelly's personal construct theory, and found that the results of his research on rigidity and dichotomous thinking was consistent with Adler's ideas.

Suicide Notes

Darbonne (1967) compared the notes written by a group of white American males who had completed suicide with simulated notes matched for race, sex, and occupation. To explore the pampered life style, Darbonne observed that the notes of completed suicides as compared to the simulated notes more often mentioned a need to have things done for them, a heightened concern with whether or not they have received emotional support from others, and the importance of parental figures for them. There were no significant differences in the difficulties experienced in adapting to loss.

There was less support for the notion that the completed suicides would be characterized by inferiority feelings and self-centered goals. There were no differences between the two sets of notes in direct expressions of low self-esteem or self-praise, feelings of being at the mercy of external forces, or in the number of self-referents. However, there were more references by the completed suicides to other persons, and there was also more mention of the absence or breaking of social ties. Darbonne felt that these last two comparisons were relevant to feelings of inferiority and self-centered goals, but they also seem related to dependency needs.

Adler had hypothesized that suicides would be very active, and Darbonne found that the completed suicides used more verbs referring to physical motor behavior than did the nonsuicidal persons, and their notes also contained more verbs and adjectives. However, the notes did not differ in length (a measure of verbal activity), and there was no difference in the method of suicide used or chosen by the subject (methods of suicide which had been rated previously by judges for the degree of activity involved).

There was some support for the notion that the completed suicides would show more veiled aggression than the nonsuicidal persons. The notes of the completed suicides had more veiled hostility, more frequent mention of the blame of others for the suicide, and more concern with informing others and addressing the note to others as compared to the notes of the nonsuicidal persons. However, the two sets of notes did not differ in expression of direct anger, mention of suffering, and feelings that others had been hurt by the past behavior of the note writer.

Overall, the results supported Darbonne's predictions based upon Adlerian ideas about suicide, with the exception of the hypothesized differences in inferiority feelings. Each idea tested by Darbonne received some support, and none of the tests produced significant results in a direction opposite to that predicted.

The eleven variables that had proved successful in differentiating the notes of the completed suicides from those of the nonsuicidal persons were used to compare the notes of those threatening suicide with those of the two other groups. With regard to veiled aggression and a pampered life style and dependency, those threatening suicide resembled the completed suicides in inferiority feelings and self-centered goals but resembled the nonsuicidal persons in activity. Those threatening suicide were divided into a high risk and a low risk group. The two groups did not differ significantly on any of the eleven variables.

Other Research

Adler stressed that suicides were psychiatrically disturbed and more similar to depressed people. He noted their feelings of inferiority and low self-esteem. He also drew attention to the aggressive motives in suicidal behavior. Research relevant to these ideas has been reviewed in detail in the chapters on psychoanalytic theory, personal construct theory and social learning theory and need not be reviewed again here. The deficiency in social interest was also examined in the chapter on personal construct theory.

Discussion

It can be seen that the problem with Adler's view of suicide is that it is not sufficiently differentiated from his view of the neurotic. Thus, most of what Adler has to say about suicidal people is applicable also to neurotics in general. Thus, research stimulated by Adlerian ideas on suicide does little more than confirm that suicidal people are psychologically disturbed. Those interested in Adler's ideas must work toward identifying characteristics of the suicidal person above and beyond those of the neurotic.

REFERENCES

Adler, A.: Suicide. *Journal of Individual Psychology*, 14:57-61, 1958.
Ansbacher, H.: Suicide. In N. Farberow & E. Shneidman (Eds.) *The cry for help*. New York: McGraw-Hill, 1961, 204-219.
Ansbacher, H.: Suicide as communication. *Journal of Individual Psychology*, 25:174-180, 1969.
Ansbacher, A.: Alfred Adler, individual psychology and Marilyn Monroe. *Psychology Today*, 1970, 3(9), 42-44, 66.
Darbonne, A.: An investigation into the communication style of suicidal individuals. *Dissertation Abstracts*, 27B:2504-2505, 1967.
Durkheim, E.: *Suicide*. Glencoe: Free Press, 1951.
Leenaars, A.A.: *Suicide notes*. New York: Human Sciences Press, 1988.
Lester, D.: Suicide and sibling position. *Individual Psychology*, 43:390-395, 1987.
Neuringer, C.: Validation of the cognitive aspect of Adler's theory of suicide. *Journal of Individual Psychology*, 1974, 30, 59-64.

Chapter 6

CARL ROGERS

CARL ROGERS (1959) proposed a simple theory of personality. He argued that the infant has an inherent tendency toward self-actualizing himself, and his behavior is directed toward satisfying this need. If this need is satisfied, he experiences pleasure. Part of the process of actualizing involves differentiation, and soon a portion of the child's experience becomes symbolized in an awareness of being. This awareness may be described as self-experience. Eventually this awareness becomes elaborated into a concept of self.

At this phase of development, the child develops a need for positive regard. This need is universal, pervasive and persistent. Rogers did not rule on whether the need is innate or learned. When the child interacts with adults, particularly, his mother, he searches for and is satisfied by love from her. The likelihood of receiving this maternal love eventually becomes more important in affecting his behavior than his need to actualize. (This sets up a conflict in the child between his need for self-actualization and his need for positive self-regard from others.)

Soon the child develops a need for positive self-regard, and whether the child feels this positive self-regard depends to a large extent on whether his parents give him positive regard. Typically, parents set up *conditions of worth*, that is, they regard the child positively only if certain conditions are met. Their regard for him is said to be conditional. As a result, the child will have positive self-regard only if he meets these conditions of worth.

In contrast, in the healthiest environment possible, a child would receive *unconditional positive regard*. The child would be prized and valued by his parents no matter what he is or does. In this case, no conditions of worth would be set up. Rogers felt that this case was hypothetically possibly, theoretically important, but never found in the real world.

Once conditions of worth are set up, then the child will begin to experience discrepancies between the conditions of worth and his actual experiences. When experiences are in accord with his conditions of worth, the child will accurately perceive and symbolize the experience. When the experiences are not in accord with the conditions of worth, his perception of the experiences may be selective and distorted. This process tends to break down the unity of the child's mind. Certain experiences tend to threaten his self. To maintain his self-concept, he has to resort to defensive maneuvers. His behavior is regulated sometimes by his self and sometimes by elements of his experience which are not included in his self. The personality becomes divided. He is no longer true to himself. For the sake of preserving the positive regard from others, he has falsified some of the values he has experienced. This is not necessarily a conscious choice.

The incongruence between his self and his experience leads to incongruities in his behavior, some of which is consistent with his self and some with experiences which have not been assimilated into his self. Experiences which are incongruent with the self and with the conditions of worth are perceived as threatening, that is, if the experience were perceived accurately, the conditions of worth would be violated. Then the need for positive self-regard would be frustrated, and the person would feel anxiety.

To minimize anxiety, the person may selectively perceive, denying to his awareness some aspects of his experience and distorting his experience in order to keep his total perception of his experience consistent with his conditions of worth. Rogers felt that this was the function of the typical psychoanalytic defense mechanisms.

Rogers's theory is very similar to the pattern of vicarious living described by Andras Angyal (1960). In the pattern of vicarious living, the individual suppresses his true self and adopts a false social self that will win acceptance and approval from his parents. This pattern arises because the parents did not love or like the child's true self. Angyal theorized that this pattern was only one of two possible patterns of disturbed behavior, the other being the pattern of noncommitment in which the person tries to make safe and predictable a world which he sees as unsafe and unpredictable. Indeed, as Angyal noted, the particular theory proposed by Rogers is the most commonly proposed theoretical concept in modern psychology and can be found, for example, in the theories of R.D. Laing and Arthur Janov.

It has proven very difficult to test Rogers's theory. Although it may be possible to assess the person's true self, it is difficult to assess his "experiences" to see if they are discrepant with this true self. Instead, researchers have studied the discrepancy between the real self (the self as the person perceives himself to be) and the ideal self (the self as the person would like to be). This discrepancy is clearly not the same as that between the true self and the conditions of worth, but it is as close as researchers can come. The general hypothesis is that the greater this discrepancy, the more psychologically disturbed the person will be. Rogers did not make specific predictions for different psychiatric syndromes, except to say that large discrepancies which arise in a brief period of time can lead to psychotic rather than neurotic breakdowns.

Self/Ideal-Self Splits in Suicidal Individuals

Norris and Makhlouf-Norris (1976) reported a large self/ideal-self discrepancy in a case study of one suicidal person. However, research on large samples has not always found significant results. Kamano and Crawford (1966) used a complex measure: the discrepancy between the actual self-concept and the least liked self-concept divided by the discrepancy between the ideal self-concept and the least liked self-concept. They found no differences between female patients who had made serious or mild attempts at suicide and nonsuicidal patients. Wilson, et al. (1969) also used a complicated measure and, in a comparison of attempted suicides, nonsuicidal psychiatric patients and normal people found that the suicidal patients and psychiatric patients both had higher discrepancies than the normal people. In a later study, they found that the self/ideal-self discrepancy was related to ratings of depression and danger to self in psychiatric patients (Miskimins, et al., 1971).

Hattem (1964) looked directly at the self-concept/ideal self-concept in individuals who had made attempts or threats at suicide and in their nonsuicidal spouses. On one set of adjectives (concerned with dominance), the suicidal people had a greater self/ideal-self discrepancy than their spouses, but on another set of adjectives (concerned with love) there were no significant differences.[1]

Discussion

It can be seen that Rogers's theory of personality is a simple one, and very little research on suicide has been conducted that is relevant to it. Furthermore, the research is not very supportive of Rogers's theory. Fu-

---

[1] We should note that some psychologists have expressed doubts as to what this self/ideal-self discrepancy actually measures (Byrne, 1966; Katz and Zigler, 1967; Kornreich, et al., 1968).

ture research on this topic should take care to include appropriate controls for depression and psychological disturbance.

It would also be interesting to explore the conditions of worth that parents might impose on their children which might facilitate the development of suicidal tendencies. For example, parents who communicate, overtly or covertly, that they wish their children had never been born (or did not deserve to exist) might well facilitate the appearance of items in the conditions of worth that the child ought to be dead, thereby increasing the likelihood of suicidal behavior in the child in later years. No research has ever been conducted on this possibility.

REFERENCES

Angyal, A.: *Neurosis and treatment*. New York: Wiley, 1965.

Byrne, D.: *An introduction to personality*. Englewood Cliffs: Prentice-Hall, 1966.

Hattem, J.: Precipitating role of discordant interpersonal relationship in suicidal behavior. *Dissertation Abstracts*, 25:1335-1336, 1964.

Kamano, D., & Crawford, C.: Self-evaluations of suicidal mental hospital patients. *Journal of Clinical Psychology*, 22:278-279, 1966.

Katz, P., & Zigler, E.: Self-image disparity. *Journal of Personality & Social Psychology*, 5:186-195, 1967.

Kornreich, L., Straka, J., & Kane, A.: Meaning of self-image disparity as measured by the Q-sort. *Journal of Consulting & Clinical Psychology*, 32:728-730.

Miskimins, R., Braucht, G., Wilson, L., & Berry, K.: Self-concept and psychiatric symptomatology. *Journal of Clinical Psychology*, 27:185-187, 1971.

Norris, H., & Makhlouf-Norris, F.: The measurement of self-identity. In P. Slater (Ed.) *Explorations of intrapersonal space*. London: Wiley, 1976.

Rogers, C.R.: A theory of therapy, personality and interpersonal relationships, as developed in the client-centered framework. In S. Koch (Ed.) *Psychology: a study of a science*. New York: McGraw-Hill, 1959, Volume 3, 184-256.

Wilson, L., Miskimins, R., Braucht, G., & Berry, K.: The severe suicide attemptor and self-concept. Unpublished, Colorado State University, 1969.

Chapter 7

HENRY MURRAY

MURRAY never proposed a theory of personality in the sense that other theorists have, though he is typically included in textbooks on the topic. Rather, Murray read the theories proposed by others and formed an amalgam of them, so that his writings are somewhat like an introduction to human behavior written in general terms. Murray accepted all theories and all points of view.

Murray (1959) listed those disciplines and theorists that had influenced his theory of personality. From Freud, Murray adopted the division of psychological forces into conscious and unconscious parts and a belief in the importance of early experiences for the development of personality. He also found the organismic, holistic or molar conceptions of personality useful, while not rejecting completely the usefulness of focussing at times on the elements that make up the whole. Murray's preference was to conceptualize the organization of the parts as hierarchical systems, with vertical integrations of superordinate and subordinate parts. Murray's analyses of the elements focussed mainly upon needs and subneeds (subordinate components of a larger system of need-aims) and dispositions (sentiments, interests, attitudes and evaluations).

Murray also emphasizes the distinction between the *needs* of the individual and the influence of the environment upon the individual, or *press*. The actual forces in the environment was called the *alpha press*, while the forces in the environment as perceived by the subject was called the *beta press*. The beta press was a better predictor of people's behavior than was the alpha press. Interestingly, Murray changed Freud's definition of cathexis from a property of the human subject to a property of the environment. He defined *cathexis* as the disposition-evoking capacity of any kind of event, that is, the capacity of an event in the environment to evoke attention, evaluation and behavior.

Murray was interested in detailing inventories of various of these concepts, and he borrowed from others for this task. For example, he listed and devised ways of measuring the fundamental needs of people. He proposed that the system of personality could be seen as composed of four subsystems, involving a psychosomatic system (needs and activities concerned with the growth and welfare of the body), a psychosexual system (needs and activities concerned with erotic love), a psychosocial system (needs and activities concerned with non-erotic social reciprocations), and a psycho-representational system (cognitive needs associated with the above systems). The personality system is composed of these systems and their subsystems and with the allocation of energy to these various component systems and subsystems.

In an early statement of his theory, Murray (1938) stressed the wholeness of humans at birth, after which they begin to self-differentiate into parts. The whole and the parts are mutually related and cannot be understood separately. Furthermore, there is a temporal unity. The history of the person *is* the person. Eventually, conflict between the parts occurs and, with increasing age, conflict resolution (that is, synthesis and creative integration back into a unified whole again).

Murray proposed that the psychic events or processes which govern our behavior at each moment in time be called regnant processes, or *regnancies*. Regnancies may be conscious or unconscious. Murray was primarily concerned with particular regnancies, the needs. He proposed classifications of needs into viscerogenic and psychogenic needs and compiled lists of the needs in each category. The viscerogenic needs (twelve in all) were classified as to whether they resulted from lacks, distensions or harms and as to whether they were positive (adient, eliciting approach) or negative (abient, eliciting avoidance). The twenty-eight psychogenic (or secondary) needs were classified as to whether they were adient, abient (approaching a liked object) or contrient (where the person approaches a disliked object). Needs often come into conflict, and Murray noted briefly that this is the cause of most neurotic disorders.

In considering the environment (which Murray also took to include the physiological processes of the body), Murray used two concepts. An object that evokes a need is said to have cathexis or be cathected. Objects that evoke positive adient needs are said to have positive cathexis and those that evoke abient or contrient needs are said to have negative cathexis.

In addition, Murray classified environmental events in terms of the kinds of benefits and harms they provided. Directional tendencies in the environment are called presses. (Neutral environmental events are *inert*.)

The press of an object is what it can do *to* the person or *for* the person. The cathexis of an object is what it can make the person do. The alpha press is the press that actually exists; the beta press is the person's interpretation of the environmental event. Murray proposed a classification of press to accompany his classification of needs. The beta press, together with the internal processes of the person, constitute the *field* (Murray and Kluckhohn, 1953).

Sequences in which press are followed by needs, thereby resulting in behavior (or in Murray's terminology, *actones*) were called *thema*. A succession of such episodes was called a *complex thema*. If a person has characteristic modes of behavior, in which certain press result in characteristic needs and characteristic behaviors, Murray referred to this as a *need integrate* or *complex*. Behaviors that result from internal needs are *proactive*, whereas those that result from external press are *reactive*.

Relevant Research

Shneidman (1980) noted that suicide can be seen as a behavior that tries to solve a problem for the person. It has a clear purpose, and we may ask "What does the act of suicide accomplish for the person?" Shneidman noted that the answer to such a question is made simpler if we have a list of the basic human needs, and he decided to use Murray's list. Shneidman suggested that a typology of suicide might parallel such a typology of needs.

Abasement: Suicide can fulfill a need to submit passively to external forces, to accept blame and to atone, or to admit inferiority.

Achievement: Suicide can accomplish something difficult, the act of killing oneself, thereby rivalling and surpassing others.

Affiliation: Suicide can fulfill the desire to join others (as in reunion suicides where the person hopes to join a deceased loved one) or to please and win the affection of significant others who still live.

Aggression: Suicide can be an act of revenge which hurts others.

Autonomy: Suicide can serve to throw off restraints, to resist coercion, to act independently and to defy convention.

Counteraction: Suicide can obliterate humiliations by resuming action, overcome weakness and fear, and maintain self-respect and pride.

Defendance: Suicide can defend the self against criticism or blame. It may justify a failure and vindicate the self.

Deference: Suicide may honor others, emulate leaders and conform to custom.

Dominance: Suicide may be an act of trying to control the human environment. The suicide may be trying to dissuade, coerce or restrain others.

Exhibition: Suicide may be designed to make an impression, to amaze and intrigue others.

Harmavoidance: Suicide is often an escape from pain.

Infaavoidance: Suicide may be a way of avoiding humiliation and escaping scorn and derision.

Inviolacy: Suicide may preserve a person's self-respect and maintain his pride.

Nurturance: Suicide may gratify the needs of others and help and protect them.

Order: Suicide may be an attempt to put things in order and to achieve balance and tidiness.

Play: Suicide may be an act of play, as in suicides that result from taking excessive risks.

Rejection: Suicide may serve to separate the person from a disliked other or to exclude and abandon someone else.

Sentience: Suicide may be a way of seeking sensuous experiences.

Sex: Suicide may further erotic feelings, both directly (in the act of hanging, for example) or romantically.

Succorance: Suicide may express a wish to be nurtured, protected and forgiven.

Understanding: Suicide may reflect a search for an answer to questions about life and death or God.

Leenaars's Formulation of Murray's Views

Leenaars (1988) identified ten components of a possible conceptualization of suicide from Murray's writings:

1. The suicide has adjustive and functional value for the person because it abolishes painful tension and provides relief from intolerable suffering.
2. The suicide is related to unsatisfied or frustrated needs, although it may be difficult for an observer to know which needs.
3. The person feels pitiful forlornness, deprivation, distress or grief.
4. The person feels extrapunitiveness (blaming others), anger, hate or physical aggression.
5. These two components (mentioned in items 3 and 4) are combined into an all-pervasive grief-rage state, coupled with dedicated, vengeful hatred that is ruling the personality.

6. There is evidence of a persistent effort to attain a specific goal.
7. There are historical, painful antecedents, such as a rejecting mother or a punishing father which are affecting the person in his current reaction.
8. There is evidence of intrapunitiveness (blaming oneself), remorse, guilt, depression, a bad conscience and a need for punishment.
9. There is evidence of egression (the person's desire to escape from the pain he is experiencing) and desertion (from his closest friends).
10. There is a state of affectlessness, that is, withdrawal, emotional dissociation, and viewing everything as purposeless and meaningless.

Leenaars found that item 3 was found more often in a sample of genuine suicide notes than in a sample of simulated suicide notes. In addition, items 1, 2, 3 and 9 were found in at least two-thirds of the genuine suicide notes.

The Edwards's Personal Preference Schedule

One psychological test was devised specially to assess fifteen of the major needs described by Murray, the Edwards's Personal Preference Schedule, but only two studies have appeared using it with suicidal individuals. Tucker and Cantor (1975) found that female attempted suicides had stronger needs for affiliation, succorance, nurturance and aggression and a weaker need for endurance as compared to peer counselors. Cantor (1976) reported that female suicide attempters had high needs for affiliation, succorance and nurturance and low needs for endurance and aggression. Suicidal ideators resembled the attempters. An item analysis suggested that the attempters needed help from others but were unable to ask for it. They could not depend on their parents for help, and their parents were a major source of their anger. They had a low threshold for pain. The ideators were similar in many respects, but they were able to ask for the help that they needed.

Several studies have looked at specific needs described by Murray, though using other psychological tests. Cross-nationally, Rudin (1968), Lester (1968) and Barrett and Franke (1970) found that measures of a society's need to achieve were not related to the suicide rates of the societies. However, studies of college students who killed themselves have suggested that they were good students who had fears of failure (Seiden, 1966), and problems with achievement motivation are often proposed to account for high rates of suicide in men (Lester, 1984) and some societies (Hendin, 1965).

A good deal of research has been conducted on the need for abasement, and the results suggest that suicidal people do have low self-esteem (Lester, 1972).

Discussion

Although some research studies appear to be relevant to Murray's proposed classification of needs, Murray did not propose a theory of suicide from which predictions can be drawn. Therefore, his theory, or more narrowly, his classification of needs, can serve only as a basis for classifying the needs fulfilled by the suicidal act and studied in research conducted on the personality of the suicidal person.

REFERENCES

Barrett, G., & Franke, R.: "Psychogenic" death. *Science*, 167:304-306, 1970.

Cantor, P.: Personality characteristics found among youthful female suicide attempters. *Journal of Abnormal Psychology*, 85:324-329, 1976.

Hendin, H.: *Suicide in Scandinavia*. New York: Doubleday, 1965.

Leenaars, A.A.: *Suicide notes*. New York: Human Sciences Press, 1988.

Lester, D.: National motives and psychogenic death rates. *Science*, 161:1260, 1968.

Lester, D.: *Why people kill themselves*. Springfield: Thomas, 1972.

Lester, D.: Suicide. In C. Widom (Eds.) *Sex roles and psychopathology*. New York: Plenum, 1984, 145-156.

Murray, H.: *Explorations in personality*. New York: Oxford, 1938.

Murray, H.: Preparations for the scaffold of a comprehensive system. In S. Koch (Ed.) *Psychology, Volume 3*. New York: McGraw-Hill, 1959, 7-54.

Murray, H., & Kluckhohn, C.: Outline of a conception of personality. In C. Kluckhohn & H. Murray (Eds.) *Personality in nature, society and culture*. New York: Knopf, 1953, 3-49.

Rudin, S.: National motives predict psychogenic death rates 25 years later. *Science*, 160:901-903, 1968.

Seiden, R.: Campus tragedy. *Journal of Abnormal Psychology*, 71:389-399, 1966.

Shneidman, E.: A possible classification of suicidal acts based on Murray's need system. *Suicide & Life-Threatening Behavior*, 10:175-181, 1980.

Tucker, D., & Cantor, P.: Personality and status profiles of peer counselors and suicide attempters. *Journal of Counseling Psychology*, 22:423-430, 1975.

Chapter 8

WILLIAM SHELDON AND HANS EYSENCK

T HE POSSIBILITY that our personality may be determined in part by our genes has long been considered by psychologists. Occasionally relationships have been hypothesized between genetically-determined physiological processes and human behavior. Some psychologists have observed differences in new-born babies and speculated that these differences were genetically caused. Occasionally, genes (usually defective) have been identified that can be shown to cause particular deviant behavior patterns.

In recent years, many studies have appeared that conclusively show the importance of genes in determining behavior. Studies of monozygotic (identical) twins raised apart from each other and compared with twins raised together have shown that genes play a role in determining behavior and personality traits. Studies of cross-fostering have shown that cross-fostered offspring show resemblances to their biological mothers, resemblances that must be mediated by genes.

However, despite these occasional studies, there have been few systematic attempts to propose physiological theories of personality. Only two major theories have been proposed in recent years, by William Sheldon and by Hans Eysenck. In this chapter, we will briefly summarize these theories and review whether they have any applicability to suicidal behavior.

William Sheldon

Sheldon (1940, 1942) proposed a theory based upon ideas that had been around at least since the writings of the ancient Greeks. Earlier writers had described three extreme types of physique. Sheldon modified this idea by rating each person for the degree of each of three components of physique: endomorphy (degree of fat), mesomorphy (degree of muscle), and ectomorphy (relative absence of both fat and muscle). For personality, Sheldon proposed three dimensions of personality (or temperament as he preferred to call it): viscerotonia (a relaxed extraversion), somatotonia (an aggressive extraversion), and cerebrotonia (a neurotic introversion).[1]

Sheldon then proposed that the genes that are responsible for our physique also determine our personality. Thus, our personality is related to our physique. The more endomorphic our physique is, the more viscerotonic our personality will be; the more mesomorphic our physique is, the more somatotonic our personality will be; and the more ectomorphic our physique is, the more cerebrotonic our personality will be.

Early research which confirmed the existence of these associations was criticized as biased. However, Parnell (1964) devised objective ways of classifying physiques, while Cortes and Gatti (1972) developed self-rating scales for personality assessment. The research conducted by Cortes and Gatti confirmed the existence of the associations predicted by Sheldon.

Of course, other explanations of the association between physique and personality can be advanced (including social shaping of and social stereotypes about physique and personality; the mediating factor of some third variable, such as the behavior of the mother toward her child, leading to both a particular physique and a corresponding personality; and the possibility that certain behaviors and personality traits may fit more easily with particular physiques).

Sheldon (1949) argued that psychological disturbance fitted into his system. Paranoids were deficient in viscerotonia, hebephrenic schizophrenics deficient in somatotonia, and manic-depressives deficient in cerebrotonia. Neurotics were similarly classified. Research supports these ideas. Schizophrenics have been found to be ectomorphic while manic-depressives were endomorphic (Rees, 1944). Cortes and Gatti (1972) found that delinquent boys were high in mesomorphy.

Applications to Suicide

Sheldon himself hypothesized that endomorphs would rarely kill themselves, while ectomorphs might be more suicidal. Few investigators have tried to link Sheldon's theory to suicidal behavior. However, some scattered research studies are pertinent here.

---

[1]These characterizations of Sheldon's dimensions of personality are mine.

Paffenbarger and Asnes (1966) found no differences in height between undergraduates who later completed suicide and those who did not. (Taller physiques would tend to be more ectomorphic, other features being equal.) Dublin and Bunzel (1933) reported that suicide was less common in men of normal weight than in men underweight or overweight. They felt that an abnormal weight might lead a person to have morbid preoccupations and increase the level of psychological disturbance. Robinson (1962) found that men who were underweight had a higher suicide rate than those of normal weight. Men fifteen percent overweight had a reduced suicide rate, those thirty-five percent overweight had a normal suicide rate, while those fifty percent overweight had a higher suicide rate.

It does seem, therefore, that the risk of completed suicide may be associated, perhaps in a complex way, with the weight of the individual. It must be noted that these studies were carried out on males. The examination of this association in females would be of interest.

In the interpretation of these studies, the possibility of *drift* should be remembered. People disposed to suicide may change physiologically as a result of their psychological state. The individual obsessed with suicide may neglect his diet and so become underweight or overweight. However, research in this area has not yet reached such levels of complexity.

One study has looked at the ratio of body length to leg length (Piney, 1935). He found that suicides had larger body lengths as compared to leg lengths than those dying from other means. Piney noted that when the body/leg length ratio was large, the aorta was often narrow, the thymus gland present, the spleen rather large, and the Malpighian bodies prominent. He hypothesized that such individuals would possess an excess of lymphatic tissue. The bodies in this study were examined after death, and so changes occurring in the dying process were not controlled for. (Piney's hypothesis with regard to a possible involvement of lymphatic tissue in completed suicides has received some support from a study by Gjukic [1957] who reported that completed suicides [and those with certain other diseases] were found to have a lymphatic constitution with reduced resistance.)

Tobias (1970) reported that suicides (and other violent and accidental deaths) had heavier brains than natural deaths, but Beskow, et al. (1976) found no differences. (Ectomorphs have a proportionately larger central nervous system than endomorphs and mesomorphs, but these two studies looked only at absolute weights.)

However, none of these studies actually measured physique in the Sheldonian manner.

Ectomorphy

Lester (1987a) used a simple measure of ectomorphy (height divided by the cube root of the weight) to assess 126 white male completed suicides. He did not have comparison figures for a nonsuicidal group, but he did find that those who died by suffocation had higher ecto-morphy scores (that is, were thinner) than those using other methods. Thomas and Greenstreet (1973) compared medical students who later killed themselves with controls and found them to have been more un-derweight, more ectomorphic, more nervously tense, heavier smokers, lighter drinkers, and lower in diastolic blood pressure.

In a cross-cultural study, Lester (1981) calculated ectomorphy ratios for typical infants and children from ten industrialized nations. Those nations with the more ectomorphic one-year olds had higher male and female suicide rates (though only the association with the male suicide rates was statistically significant). (The ectomorphy scores of the chil-dren were not related to the calorie intake, caffeine consumption or gross national product per capita of the nations.)

This finding does support Sheldon's hypothesis and is quite remark-able since it relates infant physiques to adult suicidal behavior in the na-tions. A parallel study on individuals would be most welcome.

Eysenck's Theory

One problem with Sheldon's theory is that the physiological dimen-sion that he chose for the basis of the theory (physique) is superficial. Eysenck chose a much more meaningful physiological basis for the theory, as we shall see, but it is far harder to operationally measure. This makes the theory more difficult to test.

Eysenck (1967) has argued that there are four major dimensions of personality: extraversion/introversion, neuroticism, psychoticism and intelligence. He has analyzed many studies of personality traits to show that these four dimensions continually appear as a result of factor-analyses of the personality test protocols.

In his theory he focussed on two of the dimensions: extraversion and neuroticism. Eysenck proposed that the underlying physiological basis for the dimension of neuroticism was the ease of arousability of the sym-pathetic division of the autonomic nervous system in the brain. Those with high neuroticism scores have a more active and more easily aroused sympathetic division. In a later version of the theory, Eysenck proposed that the critical brain structure underlying the determination of neuroticism was the limbic system.

For extraversion, Eysenck proposed that the ease with which the central nervous system became inhibited and the persistence of this inhibition was the underlying physiological variable. Extraverts have overly inhibited central nervous systems, while introverts have underinhibited central nervous systems. (He later pinpointed the brain structure responsible for this inhibition as the reticular activating system in the brain stem.)

This inhibition in the central nervous system of the extravert means that incoming stimuli are damped down by the time they reach the brain via the nerves from the peripheral sense organs. Thus, the extravert is relatively insensitive to stimuli, including pain. The extravert, needing a given level of central cortical activity to keep the brain at its optimal level of arousal (Lester, 1988a), therefore shows a stimulus hunger, seeking out stimuli of all kinds (varied and intense) to stimulate the cortex to the optimal level.

Eysenck argues that the extravert is more likely to smoke, have a lot of friends, be sexually active, have tattoos (and have them removed), dress brightly, and so on. In addition, since learning by classical conditioning involves the establishment of cortical electrical circuits, extraverts, with their inhibitory central nervous system, should classically condition less well. Therefore, they will not develop a conscience (or superego) as well as an introvert will since, after all, for Eysenck the conscience is nothing more than a set of classically conditioned avoidance responses.

Eysenck sees neurotics as falling into two kinds. Dysthymics (the neurotics with high levels of anxiety) are introverted neurotics, while neurotics with conversion disorders and psychopaths are extraverted neurotics.

There is much research relevant to Eysenck's theory, not all of which supports it. But this is not the place to review this research critically. Rather, it is of interest here to explore whether there is much research on suicide relevant to Eysenck's theory.

Impulsiveness

Impulsiveness is an important component in the European concept of extraversion, though not in the American concept. Various authors have stressed how impulsive suicidal individuals can be (Lester, 1972), though little psychological research has been conducted on this trait.

Lester and Wright (1973) speculated that attempted suicides were undercontrolled and completed suicides overcontrolled, using Megargee's (1966) conception of impulsiveness. However, Lester and Clopton (1979) found no differences between completed suicides and nonsuicidal psychiatric patients on Megargee's overcontrol of hostility scale.

Corder, et al. (1974) found adolescent suicide attempters to be more impulsive and to have a higher activity level than controls. Epstein, et al. (1973) compared medical students who subsequently killed themselves with those who were not suicides and found them to be rated as more impulsive.

Williams, et al. (1977) compared impulsive attempters (who acted within five minutes of thinking about suicide) with non-impulsive attempters and found no differences in age or sex. The impulsive attempters had made more prior attempts, had the means for suicide more readily accessible, and took more of the drug. The groups did not differ in their use of alcohol prior to the attempt, level of consciousness after the attempt, or chances of discovery.

Extraversion and Neuroticism

Research has consistently found, of course, that suicidal people are more psychologically disturbed than nonsuicidal individuals (Lester, 1972).

Several investigators have measured extraversion and neuroticism in suicidal individuals using Eysenck's personality tests. Koller and Castanos (1968) found that alcoholics who had a history of suicide attempts did not differ in extraversion from with those with no suicidal history, but were more neurotic. Lester (1968) found that college students who had threatened or attempted suicide obtained higher neuroticism scores than nonsuicidal students.

Colson (1972) found that student suicide attempters and ideators obtained higher neuroticism and introversion scores than the norms for the test. Irfani (1978) found that Iranian students who had thought of suicide obtained higher neuroticism, introversion and psychoticism scores than those who had not thought of suicide. In Turkey, the student suicidal ideators had higher neuroticism and psychoticism scores but did not differ in introversion. Mehryar, et al. (1977) found that student suicidal ideators had higher neuroticism and psychoticism scores but did not differ in introversion scores.

Pallis and Jenkins (1977) found that the suicidal intent was not related to neuroticism or to the sociability component of introversion in a sample of attempted suicides. However, the male attempters with low suicidal intent had higher scores on the impulsive component of extraversion. Repeaters obtained higher neuroticism scores than first-time attempters.

Paykel and Dienelt (1971) found that depressed psychiatric patients who subsequently attempted suicide did not differ in neuroticism or introversion from those who did not. Heyse, et al. (1970) found no association between introversion scores and the degree of unconsciousness in a sample of suicide attempters who used drugs for the attempt. Diekstra (1974) found no difference between attempted suicides and psychiatric controls in neuroticism or introversion. White (1974) found that adolescent suicide attempters had higher neuroticism scores but normal introversion scores.

This research is clearly not altogether consistent. Most studies find higher neuroticism scores in suicidal individuals; six studies report this while only three find no differences. Fewer studies find higher introversion scores: two studies find higher introversion scores, six find no differences, and one finds higher scores for one component of extraversion. A great deal of research needs to be done in order to clear up the reasons for the inconsistencies in this research.

Other Personality Traits

Lester (1974) pointed out that many other personality dimensions were related to Eysenck's concept of extraversion/introversion: including repression/sensitization, reducing/augmenting, field dependence/independence, thrill seeking, obsessoid/hysteroid, and eye color. Some research has looked at these dimensions.

(1) Sensitization/Repression

Eisenthal (1967) examined whether psychiatric patients who had attempted suicide, who thought about suicide, or who were nonsuicidal differed on the personality dimension of sensitization/repression. This dimension of personality was measured by noting the subjects' viewing time and liking for slides shown to them. Eisenthal found that the suicidal patients did not manifest a consistent response style to the slides. On the measure of rated tension aroused by the slides concerned with death, the suicidal ideators did appear to show repression, but on the measure of rated liking there were no differences. Furthermore, for a series of generally unpleasant slides, none of the measures significantly differentiated the groups. Eisenthal concluded that the personality dimension of repression/sensitization did not differentiate suicidal from nonsuicidal individuals.

(2) Obsessoid/Hysteroid

McDowell, et al. (1968) compared depressive patients who completed suicide with those who had not, matched for age and sex. They divided then into obsessoids, hysteroids and intermediate types, although they did not report how this was done. For the males there were no differences, but the female suicides were more likely to be classified as hysteroids than were the control patients. Vinoda (1966) compared female attempted suicides with psychiatric controls matched for age, education, marital status and social class and used the scale devised by Caine (1970) to classify the patients. There were no significant differences between the groups. Neither did these groups differ from a sample of matched medical patients. These two studies (one on completed suicides and one on attempted suicides) are inconsistent.

Murthy (1969) compared the lethal attempters and the nonlethal attempters in Vinoda's sample and found the lethal attempters to be more often obsessoids than the nonlethal attempters.

(3) Eye Color and Tattoos

Lester (1986) studied samples of white male suicides and natural deaths. The two groups did not differ in the incidence of tattoos or in eye color. Lester found that males with tattoos were more likely to use guns for their suicide, and males with brown eyes were more likely to use hanging and poison.

Psychopathic Traits

The act of suicide requires courage, inhibition of fear and anxiety, and the suppression of guilt if the act is against one's moral philosophy. Those about to kill themselves may fear the pain of the act of dying or the consequences should there be a life after death. (Jacobs [1967] has noted that suicide notes often include much content that deals with the problem of life after death. The note writer may ask the survivors to pray for him, or he may indicate that he knows God will understand.)

Spiegel and Neuringer (1963) argued and confirmed that those about to kill themselves will avoid thinking about the imminent action, and so their suicide notes will have less mention of the word "suicide."

What would facilitate the suppression of these emotions? The psychopathic individual, by definition, experiences less anxiety and guilt. Thus, we might expect to find psychopathic traits in suicidal individuals. In Eysenck's theory of psychopaths, described above, psychopaths are conceptualized as extraverted neurotics and, as such, would be less sensitive to pain. It has long been noted that adolescent females who are wrist-cutters (a mild suicidal gesture) report feeling no pain upon cutting (Graff and Mallin, 1967). Rosenthal and Rosenthal (1984) also found that some children who attempted suicide showed neither pain nor crying in response to their suicide attempt (or to other accidents), and this was especially true for those whose motives were self-punishment, escape and reunion.

For Eysenck, psychopaths classically condition very poorly (because of their inhibitory central nervous systems), and so they will not learn well from punishment and develop a conscience. They will, therefore, be relatively unsocialized.

This fits in well with the social learning theory of suicide recently proposed by Lester (1987b). In most cultures suicide is frowned upon. Indeed, in some it is a sin. Furthermore, in any culture, suicide is rare. For example, Hungary has one of the highest suicide rates in the world. Yet its rate is only about 40 per 100,000 people per year. Suicide is always a statistically deviant act.

This suggests that suicidal individuals may be nonsocialized. Those who kill themselves have not been socialized into the traditional non-suicidal culture. Thus, on psychological tests of socialization and conformity, suicidal individuals should appear to be relatively unsocialized. Of course, Durkheim's (1951) ideas on suicide include the notion that suicide would be especially common in those who were relatively poorly socially integrated and poorly socially regulated. He called these types of suicide egoistic and anomic, respectively.

The absence of adequate parenting may be an important factor here. The quality of parenting can be poor, as in disorganized families. Or one or both parents can be absent, physically or psychologically. Jacobs (1971) has documented in detail the extremely disorganized family life of suicidal teenagers.

Religion is also relevant. Membership in a religious group will act against suicidal tendencies by providing a disapproving set of values for suicide and by providing social integration for the individual. Religious participation can also substitute for, in part, inadequate parenting. Finally, religious membership is a sign that the person has been adequately socialized.

This factor (of being poorly socialized into the traditional nonsuicidal culture) is a necessary, but not sufficient factor. For the nonsocialized person, peers and role models provide a crucial input. Those who are nonsocialized will often be associated with other similarly nonsocialized people. Thus, this nonsocialized group forms its own small subculture. This subculture may share the information necessary for suicide. What methods to use? How many pills to take?

Role models, whether familiar friends or mythic heroes, provide models for nonconformity. When a Marilyn Monroe or Freddie Prinze completes suicide, they act as a role model for the ordinary person. And when one teenager in a school completes suicide, it occasionally leads to further suicides among the peer group.

The Chronic Suicide Attempter

Lester (1983) reviewed research on the person who makes repeated attempts at suicide. He concluded that the research shows them to be more often diagnosed as psychopathic or with a personality disorder, to be more often unemployed, to more often have a criminal record and to be more likely to be alcohol abusers. They seem to have a chronic maladaptive lifestyle and to be generally socially deviant.

Regional studies of attempted suicide also have found that rates are higher where indices of social disorganization are higher including overcrowding and poverty (Lester, 1983). Thus, it seems that the chronic attempter is a social deviant who comes from locales where social deviance is common. Families in these areas often fail to discipline their children and teach them the values of the larger society. They also fail to encourage them in interests and activities which would serve as deterrents to deviant behavior.

Such a child typically grows up without acquiring the attitudes and skills for achieving long-term goals. The person then turns to short-term methods for achieving goals, such as drugs, delinquent behavior, and suicide attempts. There may also be a sex difference here, with males choosing behaviors such as drugs and crime more often while females choose suicide attempts. (Females in these locales also have a high rate of illegitimate births.) A suicide attempt for such a person is a cathartic act and one which often brings about an immediate response from others.

An interesting question is why people in these locales turn to suicide rather than drugs or criminal behavior, given the predisposing factors. It may be that the choice is sex-linked as mentioned above. It may also be related to such factors as the availability of drugs in the area, the presence of a support group (or gang), and parental models.

Conformity

Little research has been done on conformity in suicidal individuals. Lester (1982) correlated the conformity scores of representative samples from various nations with the suicide rates of those nations but found no significant associations.

In studies of individuals, the MMPI has been used a lot, but the Psychopathic Deviate scale has not showed up as especially important in differentiating suicidal from nonsuicidal individuals (Lester, 1970). Perhaps a meaningful classification of suicide attempters into different types might help identify the nonsocialized type and identify his/her traits.

Religiosity

Although denomination has been studied extensively in suicidal individuals, no study has to date studied "religiosity" as a factor. In cross-regional research, Lester (1988b) has found that states with higher rates of church attendance had lower suicide rates, but this finding needs to be supplemented by studies of individuals.

Conclusion

It can be seen that physiological theories of personality have a great deal to offer the study of suicide. The theories of Sheldon and of Eysenck both suggest hypotheses for research.

Eysenck's theory, in particular, can be seen as generating a basis for a typology for suicidal individuals. In addition, his theory pulls together several disparate lines of research already conducted and provides a theoretical framework to integrate them and extend them.

REFERENCES

Beskow, J., Gottfries, C., Roos, B., & Winblad, B.: Determinants of monoamine and nonmonoamine metabolites in the human brain. *Acta Psychiatrica Scandinavia*, 53:7-20, 1976.

Caine, T.: Personality and illness. In P. Mittler (Ed.) *The psychological assessment of mental and physical handicaps.* London: Methuen, 1970, 781-817.

Colson, C.: Neuroticism, extraversion and repression-sensitization in suicidal college students. *British Journal of Social and Clinical Psychology*, 11:88-89, 1972.

Corder, B., Shorr, W., & Corder, R.: A study of social and psychological characteristics of adolescent suicide attempters in an urban disadvantaged area. *Adolescence*, 9:1-6, 1974.

Cortes, J., & Gatti, F.: *Delinquency and crime*. New York: Seminar, 1972.

Diekstra, R.: A social learning theory approach to the prediction of suicidal behavior. *Proceedings of the 7th International Congress for Suicide Prevention*. Amsterdam: Swets & Zeitlinger BV, 1974, 55-60.

Dublin, L., & Bunzel, B.: *To be or not to be*. New York: Harrison Smith & Robert Haas, 1933.

Durkheim, E.: *Suicide*. Glencoe: Free Press, 1951.

Eisenthal, S.: Suicide and aggression. *Psychological Reports*, 21:745-751, 1967.

Epstein, L., Thomas, C., Schaffer, J., & Perlin, S.: Clinical predictors of physician suicide based on medical student data. *Journal of Nervous & Mental Disease*, 156:19-29, 1973.

Eysenck, H.J.: *The biological basis of personality*. Springfield: Thomas, 1967.

Gjukic, M.: A contribution to the study of lymphatic constitution. *Z. Menschl. Vererb-U. Konstitutionslehre*, 34:303-322, 1957.

Graff, H., & Mallin, R.: The syndrome of the wrist-cutter. *American Journal of Psychiatry*, 124:36-42, 1967.

Heyse, H., Kockott, G., & Feuerlein, W.: The serious suicidal attempt. *Proceedings of the 5th International Congress for Suicide Prevention*. Vienna: IASP, 1970, 42-45.

Irfani, S.: Personality correlates of suicidal tendencies among Iranian and Turkish students. *Journal of Psychology*, 99:151-153, 1978.

Jacobs, J.: A phenomenological study of suicide notes. *Social Problems*, 15:60-72, 1967.

Jacobs, J.: *Adolescent suicide*. New York: Wiley, 1971.

Koller, K., & Castanos, J.: Attempted suicide and alcoholism. *Medical Journal of Australia*, 2:835-837, 1968.

Lester, D.: Suicide as an aggressive act. *Journal of General Psychology*, 79:83-86, 1968.

Lester, D.: Attempts to predict suicidal risk using psychological tests. *Psychological Bulletin*, 74:1-17, 1970.

Lester, D.: *Why people kill themselves*. Springfield: Thomas, 1972.

Lester, D.: *A physiological basis for personality traits*. Springfield: Thomas, 1974.

Lester, D.: Ectomorphy and suicide. *Journal of Social Psychology*, 113:135-136, 1981.

Lester, D.: Conformity, suicide and homicide. *Behavior Science Research*, 17:24-30, 1982.

Lester, D.: *Why people kill themselves*. Springfield: Thomas, 1983.

Lester, D.: Tattoos, eye color and method for suicide. *Activitas Nervosa Superior*, 28:239-240, 1986.

Lester, D.: Ectomorphy ratios of completed suicides. *Perceptual & Motor Skills*, 64:86, 1987a.

Lester, D.: *Suicide as a learned behavior*. Springfield: Thomas, 1987b.

Lester, D.: A systems theory of personality. *Psychological Reports*, 1988a.

Lester, D.: Religiosity and personal violence. *Journal of Social Psychology*, 1988b.

Lester, D., & Clopton, J.: Suicide and overcontrol. *Psychological Reports*, 44:758, 1979.

Lester, D., & Wright, T.: Suicide and overcontrol. *Psychological Reports*, 32:1278, 1973.

McDowall, A.W., Brooke, E., Freeman-Browne, D., & Robin, A.: Subsequent suicide in depressed inpatients. *British Journal of Psychiatry*, 114:749-754, 1968.

Megargee, E.: Undercontrolled and overcontrolled personality types in extreme anti-social aggression. *Psychological Monographs*, 80:#3, 1966.

Mehryar, A., Hekmat, H., & Khajavi, R.: Some personality correlates of contemplated suicide. *Psychological Reports*, 40:1291-1294, 1977.

Murthy, V.: Personality and the nature of suicide attempts. *British Journal of Psychiatry*, 115:791-795, 1969.

Pallis, D., & Jenkins, J.: Extraversion, neuroticism and intent in attempt suicide. *Psychological Reports*, 41:19-22, 1977.

Paffenbarger, R., & Asnes, D.: Chronic disease in former college students. *American Journal of Public Health*, 59:900-908, 1969.

Parnell, R.: Simplified somatotypes. *Journal of Psychosomatic Research*, 8:311-315, 1964.

Paykel, E., & Dienelt, M.: Suicide attempts following acute depression. *Journal of Nervous & Mental Disease*, 153:234-243, 1971.

Piney, A.: A peculiar bodily disproportion. *Lancet*, 2:972, 1935.

Rees, L.: Physical constitution, neurosis and psychosis. *Proceedings of the Royal Society of Medicine*, 37:635-638, 1944.

Robinson, P.: Suicide. *Postgraduate Medicine*, 32:154-159, 1962.

Rosenthal, P., & Rosenthal, S.: Suicidal behavior by preschool children. *American Journal of Psychiatry*, 141:520-525, 1984.

Sheldon, W.: *The varieties of human physique*. New York: Harper, 1940.

Sheldon, W.: *The varieties of temperament*. New York: Harper, 1942.

Sheldon, W.: *Varieties of delinquent youth*. New York: Harper, 1949.

Spiegel, D., & Neuringer, C.: Role of dread in suicidal behavior. *Journal of Abnormal & Social Psychology*, 66:507-511, 1963.

Thomas, C., & Greenstreet, R.: Psychobiological characteristics in youth as predictors of five disease states. *John Hopkins Medical Journal*, 132:16-43, 1973.

Tobias, P.: Brain-size, grey matter and race. *American Journal of Physical Anthropology*, 32:3-26, 1970.

Vinoda, K.: Personality characteristics of attempted suicide. *British Journal of Psychiatry*, 112:1143-1150, 1966.

White, H.: Self-poisoning in adolescents. *British Journal of Psychiatry*, 124:24-35, 1974.

Williams, C., Sale, I., & Wignell, A.: Correlates of impulsive suicidal behavior. *New Zealand Medical Journal*, 85:323-325, 1977.

Chapter 9

CONCLUSIONS

A N EFFORT has been made in this book to review some of the classic psychological theories of the human mind and of human behavior and to explore what relevance these theories have for understanding suicide. It can be seen that several theories have much to contribute to an understanding of suicide and can shape the questions to be addressed by future research. Three theories stand out in this regard: social learning theory and the theories proposed by Sigmund Freud and Hans Eysenck. All three of these theories explain many of the research findings reported on suicidal people and have relevance for many of the phenomena investigated by researchers.

It is this breadth that makes the classical psychological theories more useful than specific psychological theories proposed by suicidologists to account for suicidal behavior. For example, to propose that suicide is most common in those who are hopeless is an important proposition and has generated some supportive research (Lester, 1983). However, such a proposition explains only the relationship between hopelessness and suicide. It has little applicability to other research findings.

Let me illustrate this by proposing seven specific theories of suicidal behavior. Several of these are modelled on the theories of drug abuse presented in Lettieri, et al. (1980). Others are hypotheses that I have thought of myself. After presenting these theories, I will compare them with the classic psychological theories reviewed in this book.

A Physiological Theory of Suicide

It seems quite unlikely that a specific genetic factor will be found for suicide. Suicide is typically associated with psychiatric illness, and studies to explore the inheritance of suicidal tendencies have always failed to tease out the confounding effect of psychiatric illness. For example, twin studies of suicide have not assessed the role of psychiatric disturbance in the completed suicides (Lester, 1985).

Research into the brains of suicides also runs up against the same problem. Those physiological features identified for suicidal people are typically characteristic of depressives in general (Lester, 1983).

Thus, what is critical for an organic model of suicide is to suggest factors that may be unique to the suicidal individual rather than characteristic of psychiatrically disturbed people in general. It is possible to suggest several factors that might be relevant.

First, the act of suicide requires courage, inhibition of fear and anxiety, and the suppression of guilt (if the act is against one's moral philosophy). Those about to complete suicide may fear the pain of the act of dying or the consequences should there be a life after death. Jacobs (1967) has noted that suicide notes often include much to deal with the problem of life after death. The note writer may ask the survivors to pray for them, or he may indicate that he knows that God will understand his act.

What would facilitate suppression of emotions? The psychopath, by definition, experiences less shame, guilt and remorse. Thus we might expect to find psychopathic traits in suicidal individuals, and there are several organic theories of psychopathy (see, for example, Lester, 1974). In addition, it may be that suicidal individuals (especially those who repeat suicidal acts) are less sensitive to pain. Such people have been called reducers (Petrie, 1967) or extraverts (Eysenck, 1967). Spiegel and Neuringer (1963) have argued that those about to complete suicide will avoid thinking about the imminent action and so their suicide notes will have less mention of suicide. The personality style of repression (Bryne, 1961) would facilitate such a tactic.

Second, there may be physiological factors that resist succumbing to the mode chosen for suicide. It has been suggested that females are physiologically more resistant than males to psychic trauma, a factor which may in part account for the fact that more females survive suicidal actions (Lester, 1984). For example, in falls, females are more likely to survive (Robertson, et al., 1978).

Other similar factors may include an "allergic" reaction to drugs, so that the person is more likely to vomit after an ingestion. Or perhaps a higher threshold for succumbing to their effects. (Sheldon [1942], for example, argued that cerebrotonics were more resistant to the effects of various drugs such as sedatives and hypnotics.)

An Existential Theory of Suicide

Often people have difficulty meeting the demands or expectations placed upon them by society (or by themselves). This can result in conflict, and the resulting emotion of this conflict may be anxiety. If this anxiety is accompanied by a belief that one is powerless to affect one's environment (a felling of helplessness) and thereby to eliminate the source of the stress, then the person will probably experience low self-esteem. Not many options remain open for such an individual.

As Gold (1980) has pointed out, such an individual may turn to drug use as a means of reducing the anxiety. However, other tension-relieving tactics exist. Those who have talked to wrist-cutters, for example, have reported how the feelings of tension build up in the patient until, on cutting the wrists and seeing the blood flow, the tension drains way (Graff and Mallin, 1967). Often the patient reports an absence of pain under this state of intense tension.

The existential position sees suicide as a tactic in which the person assumes control of his or her life. By the act of the suicide, the individual responds, behaves, becomes fully human. Indeed, Binswanger (1958), in discussing the case of Ellen West, an anorexic female, concluded that "only in her decision for death did she find herself and choose herself. The festival of death was the festival of the birth of her existence" (p. 298).

Thus, under conditions of external demands and a feeling of powerlessness, suicide may be a behavior that resolves the conflict, reduces the anxiety and relieves the feelings of powerlessness. Such a theory may explain why some people make repeated attempts at suicide. These repeaters appear to differ in personality from one-time attempters (Lester, 1983). For example, Alvarez (1972) discussed the suicide of Sylvia Plath, the American poet, and suggested that her third attempt (as a result of which she died) was not intended by Plath to be fatal.

A Personality Factor Relevant for Suicide

Many personality factors have been suggested as being particularly relevant to suicide. Lester (1983), for example, has noted depression and a sense of hopelessness, belief in an external locus of control, neuroticism, alienation, low self-esteem, and a propensity for risk taking as traits likely to be found in the suicidal individual.

These traits are all easily measured by psychological inventories currently available. An interesting personality variable that may also be associated with the suicidal personality (though less easily measured) has been suggested by Khantzian (1978). Khantzian has described an ego-function which he has called self-care and self-regulation. These ego-functions include signal-anxiety, reality-testing, good judgment, and adequate self-control. It is possible that the suicidal individual has a defect in these self-care functions. The suicidal person may not anticipate, perceive or appreciate the danger in the things that he does and in the life-style he chooses. This is especially true of the suicide attempter, who may repeatedly make life-threatening gestures which are harmful (though not lethal) to himself. Suicidal people are frequently found to be violent and assaultive, more likely to abuse drugs and alcohol, and more likely to have committed crimes than nonsuicidal people (Lester, 1983). They show a general tendency to harm themselves, indicating a chronic failure in self-care and self-regulation.

Why have these people failed to develop these important ego-functions? Khantzian saw the cause to be a failure to adopt and internalize these functions from caring parents in early and subsequent phases of development, most likely because the parents overly deprived (frustrated) or indulged the child.

If the infant, on the other hand, experiences good mothering, then he can internalize these qualities and functions from the parents, thereby developing an ability to care for himself. (Incidentally, he will probably also develop an ability to relate more intimately with others and a secure sense of his own value, both of which will make suicide less likely in later life.)

Psychotherapists frequently focus on this issue with their patients. However, caring for oneself has been typically defined narrowly by psychological researchers to mean valuing oneself, or having high self-esteem. Caring for oneself can also mean taking care of oneself, however, and this has been ignored on the whole by researchers.

A Deindividuation Theory of Suicide

There are two conceptual approaches to the concept of deindividuation (Dipboye, 1977). Deindividuation refers to the process of losing one's distinctiveness or individuality. According to the first viewpoint, deindividuation reduces moral constraints, thereby releasing random, irrational and destructive behavior. Such an experience may not be undesirable, for the person may enjoy engaging in these new behaviors. The second approach proposes that people actively seek a separate and unique identity. A loss of identity arouses negative affect and a renewed search for an individual identity. Dipboye compares these two views with the invisible men of H.G. Wells (whose invisible man sought the anomity of the mass movement) and of Ralph Ellison (whose invisible man searched for an identity that a racist society had denied him).

The notion of deindividuation leading to a loss of restraint stems from the ideas of Freud (1960) and Jung (1946) and has been developed by Zimbardo (1969). This conception, however, appears to have little usefulness for a theory of suicide.

The notion of deindividuation as an unpleasant experience that motivates a search for identity has more potential as an explanation for suicide. Dipboye defines identity seeking as a set of behaviors that are instrumental in affirming the identity of a person who has been deindividuated.

Fromm (1956) has pointed out the dilemma here. People want both a separate identity while also escaping from the feeling of separateness. It is important to belong while feeling unique. Dipboye noted that one consequence of deindividuation can be aggression, aggression whose aim is to achieve reindividuation.

If an external source is seen as responsible for the person's deindividuation, then the aggression may well be directed outward, as assaultive or murderous acts. The assassination of John Kennedy by Lee Harvey Oswald can perhaps be viewed in this light (Progoff, 1967). However, if the person feels that he is mainly responsible for the deindividuation, then the aggression may well be directed inward, resulting in suicidal behavior.

Klapp (1969) has described a process which he named "ego screaming" in which the person seeks an audience and tries to draw attention to himself. The critical goal may be attention rather than approval. This process seems applicable to suicides which take place in public places and which may involve city officials (such as police officers) and the news media, such as Japanese seppuku or some jumpers from bridges and buildings, and some murder-suicide incidents.

Dipboye noted that the search for an identity may lead to anti-conformity (rather than more passive nonconformity) and risk-taking. Both of these consequences may facilitate suicidal behavior.

The Paradox of Depression and Suicide

Among the many theories of depression, two are the focus for this theory of suicide. First, depression is often characterized by a sense of hopelessness, powerlessness and futility. Seligman (1975) proposed a learned helplessness model of depression, in which he asserted that the component symptoms of depression are consequences of the person having learned that outcomes are uncontrollable. If you learn that there is no relationship between what you do and the outcomes, then you give up responding because you feel helpless.

Second, Beck (1967) proposed a model of depression in which a salient feature is that depressed people tend to accept personal responsibility for failures and negative outcomes. Such beliefs may in some cases approach delusional proportions. This self-blame often leads to desires for self-punishment. Beck has shown that these symptoms of depression increase with the depth (severity) of the depression.

Abramson and Sackeim (1977) have pointed out that these two models, if combined, constitute a paradox. The paradoxical situation is that individuals who are depressed are blaming themselves for outcomes that they believe they neither caused nor controlled.

Abramson and Sackeim explored various possible resolutions of this paradox. Two are of interest to a theory of suicide. One possible resolution is that there are two groups of depressives. Each group could be characterized by one of the opponent features of the paradox. They noted that no single study has examined the covariation of the two kinds of symptoms in a single sample of clinically depressed patients.

A second possible resolution is that, indeed, people do exist with internal inconsistencies (of which they may or may not be aware). The externally perceived (by others) paradox is a result of an internal inconsistency in the patient.

This leaves us with four possible types of depressives: those with only one of the two component symptoms of the paradox, those with neither, and those with both. When we turn to the issue of suicide, it can be seen that patients with both component symptoms of the paradox may be especially likely to contemplate suicide. Patients who feel both blameworthy and who simultaneously feel helpless may be especially prone to see suicide as the only response in the life situation. Patients with only one of the component symptoms still have other options. Those feeling blameworthy but who feel in control have the option of considering possible nonsuicidal effective tactics. Those feeling helpless but not blameworthy have an external source to blame for their misery (and so may be expected to feel angry at others, thereby reducing the desire to harm themselves.

Other writers have seen the suicidal person as thinking rigidly, in either-or dichotomies, and irrationally (Neuringer, 1964; Shneidman and Farberow, 1957). These thinking characteristics may increase the dangerousness of the depression paradox for the potentially suicidal person with both component symptoms.

Thus, the depression paradox theory of suicide proposes that suicidal behavior will be especially likely in those depressed individuals who show both components of the paradox.

A Family Process Theory of Adolescent Suicide Attempts

A theory of suicide could focus on the family from which the suicidal individual comes, rather than the individual himself. In this perspective the family becomes the patient. In proposing a family process theory of juvenile drug addiction, Coleman (1980) suggested that the families experience a high incidence of traumatic events connected with premature deaths, losses and separations which are not effectively mourned or otherwise resolved. The death or loss is not in itself the critical event, but rather the family interactions that result in unsuccessful mourning.

A review of the literature on loss in suicides revealed some inconsistencies (Lester, 1983). About half of the studies find no excess of loss in the childhoods of suicides as compared to other pathological groups, while the remaining studies find an excess. It is reasonable, therefore, to assume that loss is a problem for families with potentially suicidal children.

Coleman did not explain how an incomplete mourning process leads to drug addiction in a child, but she did point to parallels between drug addiction and death: early drug use symbolizes imminent death, removal from the home to a treatment facility symbolizes the funeral, and family treatment symbolizes resurrection. Attempted suicide in an adolescent produces a much closer parallel to death. When the adolescent in a family attempts suicide, the family can re-experience and work through an event very similar to previous losses in the family. The ineffectiveness of the family in working through such losses adequately may result in the adolescent making repeated suicide attempts, and the family shows what might be called a repetition compulsion. The suicidal adolescent member of the family perhaps martyrs him/herself in order to fulfill the family's need for a death (see Stanton [1977] for this view of the juvenile drug addict).

Again, in discussing the juvenile addict, Coleman pointed to the likelihood that adolescent drug use is facilitated by the conflicts over separation that are intensified during adolescence. A similar problem can be seen in the suicidal family, especially since the suicide attempt threatens death (a separation), but results in the family showing concern about the problem adolescent (reunion). It is likely that adolescent suicide attempts are intimately related to the issue of separation from the parents. Separation at this time may be especially difficult if earlier losses were incompletely or ineffectively mourned.

Coleman suggested that the absence of a religious orientation in a family may increase the likelihood of an adolescent becoming an addict. The absence of a religious orientation makes mourning more difficult. A sense of family hopelessness and lack of purpose or meaning contributes to deviant patterns of responding in the family members. The absence of a religious orientation and a lack of purpose or meaning in the family philosophy may similarly contribute to suicidal behavior in adolescent members of problem families, particularly since depression and hopelessness are so closely related to an increased risk of suicide.

Thus, it can be seen that Coleman's theory of adolescent drug use can be easily applied to adolescent suicide attempts.

Predispositional and Situational Factors in Suicide

This theory proposes an interactional view of the causation of suicide. An important predisposing factor in suicide is the degree of access to the methods for suicide. Recent research by Lester and Murrell (1982) has shown that states with the strictest handgun control laws had lower suicide rates by firearms and, indeed, lower suicide rates overall. Experience in Australia has shown that reducing the size of prescriptions for drugs and enclosing the pills in plastic blisters has dramatically reduced the incidence of self-poisoning with these drugs (Stoller, 1969). There is also some evidence, though presently in dispute, that detoxification of domestic gas in the United Kingdom may have reduced the suicide (Kreitman, 1976).

This factor of access has been used to account for the overwhelming use of guns by police officers who complete suicide (Danto, 1978) and their high suicide rate (since guns are a more lethal method for suicide than other methods), and the use by doctors and nurses of medications.

Access to the preferred method for suicide has long been an important variable for suicide lethality on prediction scales (Lester, 1973).

A second important predisposing factor for suicide is the prevailing degree of tolerance toward suicide in the culture. Dublin and Bunzel (1933) first suggested this factor, but it has continually been proposed as an etiological factor, for example, by Farber (1968) and by Henderson and Williams (1974).

To some extent this factor feeds into a cycle. If a society has a tolerant attitude toward suicide, then suicide may well become more common. But then as suicide becomes more common, the society becomes used to, familiar with and accepting of suicide.

The crucial predisposing factor for suicide, however, is the possession of particular personality traits. This factor is critical, for many people in a society have access to the means for suicide, and almost all are aware of the attitude of the society toward suicide. The fact that only a few of the members of the society complete suicide suggests that the individual personality traits must play the critical role.

What are these personality traits? First, the presence of psychiatric disorders, in particular depression, seems to be important. The evidence appears to indicate that the presence of a psychiatric depression increases the likelihood of suicide as the cause of death by a factor of fifteen (Lester, 1983).

Secondly, there appear to be particular personality traits that may predispose a person to complete suicide. A recent review of research pointed to low self-esteem, neuroticism, introversion, a belief in an external locus of control, alienation and a risk-taking propensity (Lester, 1983).

The theory has been applied so far to completed suicide, but it can also be applied to attempted suicide. The access to the means for suicide is no different for completed and attempted suicide. However, societal attitudes may affect the choice of behaviors. For example, society perceives attempted suicide as a "feminine" behavior and completed suicide as a "masculine" behavior (Linehan, 1973), and this has been used to account for the sex difference in the outcome of suicidal actions (Lester, 1979). Furthermore, the personality traits of completed suicides and attempted suicides may be different. Several authors have noted that those who make repeated suicide attempts are more likely to have personality disorders than other suicidal groups (Lester, 1983).

Discussion

It can be seen that the theories proposed above are quite limited in range. Several propose a single personality (or physiological) trait as important for understanding suicide. Others propose two variables. For example, the final theory proposed above (Predisposition And Situational Factors In Suicide) suggests an interaction of a personality trait and the availability of methods for suicide. This particular theory has, in fact, already served as the theoretical basis for a paper on suicide (Lester, 1987). Lester found that the availability of guns in the states of the USA (measured by the strictness of state handgun control laws) and the moral acceptability of suicide (measured by the religiosity of the people as evidenced by their church attendance) accounted for 46 percent of the variation in the states' suicide rates.

Other similar theories that have been proposed. Farber (1968) in his "Theory Of Suicide" hypothesized that suicide was more likely if there were heavy demands on the individual for competence and interpersonal giving, if suicide is morally acceptable, if the individual has few resources and if hopelessness is high. Four variables. Two personality traits and two situational variables.

In contrast, Freud's psychoanalytic theory provides a causal framework for suicide since it includes developmental experiences (loss and frustration) in the causation of suicide. It suggests several current personality traits as pertinent (depression and anger) and raises the question of how suicides cope with their anger (punishment experiences in childhood). It suggests precipitating causes for suicidal behavior (real or imagined loss). It points out the parallels with other destructive and self-destructive behaviors (homicide and indirect self-destructive behaviors such as drug abuse). And finally, it prods the researcher to look beyond the superficial circumstances to seek unconscious determinants. The theory provides a much richer understanding of suicidal behavior than the more limited theories proposed in this section.

Of course, it may be that, in the future, suicidologists will be able to combine many of these mini-theories together into broader theories. However, it is likely to prove more fruitful if these mini-theories could be firmly rooted in the classic psychological theories of human behavior.

REFERENCES

Abramson, L., & Sackheim, H.: A paradox in depression. *Psychological Bulletin*, 84:838-851, 1977.
Alvarez, A.: *The savage God*. New York: Random House, 1972.
Beck, A.T.: *Depression*. New York: Harper & Row, 1967.
Binswanger, L.: The case of Ellen West. In R. May, E. Angel, & H. Ellenberger (Eds.) *Existence*. New York: Basic, 1958, 237-364.

Byrne, D.: The repression-sensitization scale. *Journal of Personality*, 29:334-349, 1961.

Coleman, S.: Incomplete mourning and addict/family transactions. In D. Lettieri, M. Sayers, & H. Pearson (Eds.) *Theories on drug abuse*. Washington, DC: NIDA, 1980, 83-89.

Danto, B.: Police suicide. *Police Stress*, 1(1):32-40, 1978.

Dipboye, R.: Alternative approaches to deindividuation. *Psychological Bulletin*, 84:1057-1075, 1977.

Dublin, L.I., & Bunzel, B.: *To be or not to be*. New York: Harrison Smith, 1933.

Eysenck, H.J.: *The biological basis of personality*. Springfield: Thomas, 1967.

Farber, M.L.: *Theory of suicide*. New York: Funk & Wagnalls, 1968.

Freud, S.: *Group psychology and the analysis of the ego*. New York: Bantam, 1960.

Fromm, E.: *The art of loving*. New York: Harper & Row, 1956.

Gold, S.: The CAP control theory of drug abuse. In D. Lettieri, M. Sayers, & H. Pearson (Eds.) *Theories on drug abuse*. Washington, DC: NIDA, 1980, 8-11.

Graff, H., & Mallin, R.: The syndrome of the wrist cutter. *American Journal of Psychiatry*, 124:36-42, 1967.

Henderson, S., & Williams, C.: On the prevention of suicide. *Australian & New Zealand Journal of Psychiatry*, 8:237-240, 1974.

Jacobs, J.: A phenomenological study of suicide notes. *Social Problems*, 15:60-72, 1967.

Jung, C.: *Psychological types or the psychology of individuation*. New York: Harcourt Brace, 1946.

Khantzian, E.: The ego, the self and opiate addiction. *International Review of Psychoanalysis*, 5:189-198, 1978.

Klapp, P.: *Collective search for identity*. New York: Holt, Rinehart & Winston, 1969.

Kreitman, N.: The coal gas story. *British Journal of Preventive & Social Medicine*, 30:86-93, 1976.

Lester, D.: The physician and suicide. *Sandorama*, #2:19-21, 1973.

Lester, D.: *A physiological basis for personality traits*. Springfield: Thomas, 1974.

Lester, D.: Sex differences in suicidal behavior. In E. Gomberg & V. Franks (Eds.) *Gender and disordered behavior*. New York: Brunner/Mazel, 1979, 287-300.

Lester, D.: *Why people kill themselves*. Springfield: Thomas, 1983.

Lester, D.: Suicide. In C.S. Widom (Ed.) *Sex roles and psychopathology*. New York: Plenum, 1984, 145-150.

Lester, D.: Genetics, twin studies and suicide. *Suicide & Life-Threatening Behavior*, 16:274-285, 1986.

Lester, D.: An availability-acceptability theory of suicide. *Activitas Nervosa Superior*, 29:164-166, 1987.

Lester, D., & Murrell, M.: The preventive effect of strict gun control laws on suicide and homicide. *Suicide & Life-Threatening Behavior*, 12:131-140, 1982.

Lettieri, D., Sayers, M., & Pearson, H.: (Eds.) *Theories on drug abuse*. Washington, DC: NIDA, 1980.

Linehan, M.: Suicide and attempted suicide. *Perceptual & Motor Skills*, 37:31-34, 1973.

Neuringer, C.: Rigid thinking in suicidal individuals. *Journal of Consulting Psychology*, 28:54-58, 1964.

Petrie, A.: *Individuality in pain and suffering*. Chicago: University of Chicago Press, 1967.

Progoff, I.: The psychology of Lee Harvey Oswald. *Journal of Individual Psychology*, 23:37-47, 1967.

Robertson, H., Lakshminargan, S., & Hudson, L.: Lung injury following a 50 meter fall into water. *Thorax*, 33:175-180, 1978.

Seligman, M.: *Helplessness*. San Francisco: Freeman, 1975.

Shneidman, E.S., & Farberow, N.L.: The logic of suicide. In E.S. Shneidman & N.L. Farberow (Eds.) *Clues to suicide*. New York: McGraw-Hill, 1957, 31-40.

Sheldon, W.: *The varieties of temperament*. New York: Harper, 1942.

Spiegel, D., & Neuringer, C.: Role of dread in suicidal behavior. *Journal of Abnormal & Social Psychology*, 66:507-511, 1963.

Stanton, M.: The addict as savior. *Family Process*, 16:191-197, 1977.

Stoller, A.: Suicide and attempted suicides in Australia. *Proceedings of the 5th International Conference on Suicide Prevention*. London: IASP, 1969.

Zimbardo, P.: The human choice. In W. Arnold & D. Levine (Eds.) *17th Nebraska Symposium on motivation*. Lincoln: University of Nebraska, 1969.

AUTHOR INDEX

SUBJECT INDEX

A

Accidents, motor vehicle, 59
Achievement motivation, 97
Airplane accidents, 59
Aggression, 15, 84, 87, 88
Alcohol abuse, 11, 31, 35, 104
Allergies, 114
Anger, 26, 72
Anomie, 3, 35, 84, 107
Anxiety, 8, 90, 115
Approval of suicide, 120
Army, 43
Attempted suicide, 36, 37, 45
Availability of methods, 120

B

Birth order, 86
Biochemical analyses, 5
Bridges, 53, 60

C

Catalogic, 74
Childhood, 86
Classical conditioning, 23, 44, 107
Clusters of suicide, 60
Cognitive therapy, 27
Conditions of worth, 89
Conformity, 109
Conscience, 7
Constriction, 73, 76
Constructs, 70
Coping skills, 44
Crime, 35

D

Death instinct, 10
Defense mechanisms, 9, 90
Deindividuation, 116
Depression, 14, 25, 30, 73, 76, 87, 91
Depression paradox, 117
Deprivation, 8
Derivative desires, 8, 72
Dichotomous thinking, 75, 86
Diagnoses, 4
Direct decision therapy, 28
Drug abuse, 11, 31, 119

E

Ectomorphy, 100, 102, 114
Edwards Personal Preference Schedule, 97
Ego, 7
Egoistic suicide, 3, 35, 84, 107
Ego-ideal, 7
Ego-splitting, 9, 49
Ellison, Ralph, 117
Epidemics of suicide, 59
Existentialism, 115
External constraints, 12, 41
Extraversion, 104, 114
Eye color, 106

F

Family dynamics, 49, 119
Fatalistic suicide, 72, 77
Fetishism, 23
Firearms, 54, 120
Focal suicide, 11

131